Bernard of Clairvaux On the Spirituality of Relationship

by
John R. Sommerfeldt

THE NEWMAN PRESS
New York/Mahwah, N.J.

Cover design by Cynthia Dunne

Book design by Celine Allen

The typeface used for chapter titles in this book is Clairvaux.

Library of Congress Cataloging-in-Publication Data

Sommerfeldt, John R.
  Bernard of Clairvaux on the spirituality of relationship / by John R. Sommerfeldt.
    p. cm.
  Includes bibliographical references and index.
  ISBN 0-8091-4253-8 (alk. paper)
  1. Bernard, of Clairvaux, Saint, 1090 or 91–1153. 2. Bernard, of Clairvaux, Saint, 1090 or 91–1153—Contributions on the spirituality of relationship. 3. Spiritual life—Catholic Church. I. Title.

  BX4700.B5S65 2004
  271'.1202—dc22

                                                                    2004004395

Published by
THE NEWMAN PRESS
An imprint of Paulist Press
997 Macarthur Boulevard
Mahwah, New Jersey 07430

www.paulistpress.com

Printed and bound in the United States of America

Contents

To

the memory of

PASCHAL PHILLIPS

monk of Gethsemani Abbey

faithful, far-sighted minister
to his monastery and order

compassionate and creative servant
of children and of the
weak and poor

and

my best friend

Table of Abbreviations

General Abbreviations

ASOC
Analecta Sacri Ordinis Cisterciensis; Analecta Cisterciensia. Roma, 1945–.

Bernard de Clairvaux
Bernard de Clairvaux. Commission d'histoire de l'Ordre de Cîteaux, 3. Paris: Editions Alsatia, 1953.

Bernardus Magister
John R. Sommerfeldt (ed.). *Bernardus Magister: Papers Presented at the Nonacentenary Celebration of the Birth of Saint Bernard of Clairvaux, Kalamazoo, Michigan, Sponsored by the Institute of Cistercian Studies, Western Michigan University, 10–13 May 1990.* Cistercian Studies 135. Kalamazoo, Michigan: Cistercian Publications; Saint Nicolas-lès-Cîteaux: Cîteaux: Commentarii Cistercienses, 1992.

Bernhard von Clairvaux
Joseph Lortz (ed.). *Bernhard von Clairvaux, Mönch und Mystiker: Internationaler Bernhardkongress, Mainz 1953.* Veröffentlichungen des Instituts für europäische Geschichte Mainz, 6. Wiesbaden: Franz Steiner Verlag GmbH, 1955.

CF
Cistercian Fathers [series]. Spencer, Massachusetts; Washington, D.C.; Kalamazoo, Michigan: Cistercian Publications, 1970–.

Cîteaux
Cîteaux in de Nederlanden; Cîteaux: Commentarii cistercienses, 1950–.

Coll
Collectania o.c.r.; Collectania Cisterciensia, 1934–.

CS
Cistercian Studies [series]. Spencer, Massachusetts; Washington, D.C.; Kalamazoo, Michigan: Cistercian Publications, 1969–.

CSQ   *Cistercian Studies* [periodical]; *Cistercian Studies Quar-*
                      terly, 1961–.

James   Bruno Scott James (trans.). *The Letters of St. Bernard of*
                      Clairvaux. London: Burns Oates, 1953. Reprinted Kala-
                      mazoo, Michigan: Cistercian Publications, 1998.

Luddy   *St. Bernard's Sermons for the Seasons & Principal Festivals*
                      of the Year. Trans. A Priest of Mount Melleray [Ailbe J.
                      Luddy]. Reprint, Westminster, Maryland: The Carroll
                      Press, 3 vols., 1950.

PL   J.-P. Migne (ed.). Patrologia latina. Paris: apud J.-P. Migne
                      editorem, 221 vols., 1841.

RB   *Regula monachorum sancti Benedicti.*

Sint Bernardus   *Sint Bernardus van Clairvaux: Gedenkboek door monniken*
van Clairvaux   *van de noord- en zuidnederlandse cisterciënser abdijen*
                      samengesteld bij het achtste eeuwfeest van Sint Bernardus'
                      dood, 20 Augustus 1153–1953. Rotterdam: N.V. Uitgeverij
                      De Forel, 1953.

Spiritual   John R. Sommerfeldt. *The Spiritual Teachings of Bernard*
Teachings   *of Clairvaux.* An Intellectual History of the Early Cister-
                      cian Order, [1]. Cistercian Studies 125. Kalamazoo,
                      Michigan: Cistercian Publications, 1991.

The Works of Bernard of Clairvaux

SBOp   Jean Leclercq et al. (eds.). *Sancti Bernardi opera.* Roma:
                      Editiones Cistercienses, 8 vols. in 9, 1957–1977.

Abb   *Sermo ad abbates*

Apo   *Apologia ad Guillelmum abbatem*

Asspt   *Sermo in assumptione B.V.M.*

Conv   *Sermo ad clericos de conversione*

Csi   *De consideratione*

Ded   *Sermo in dedicatione ecclesiae*

Dil   *De diligendo Deo*

Div	*Sermo de diversis*
Ep	*Epistola*
Gra	*De gratia et libero arbitrio*
4 HM	*Sermo in feria IV hebdomadae sanctae*
Hum	*De gradibus humilitatis et superbiae*
JB	*Sermo in nativitate sancti Ioannis Baptistae*
Mal	*Sermo in transitu sancti Malachiae episcopi*
Mart	*Sermo in festivitate sancti Martini episcopi*
Mich	*Sermo in festo sancti Michaëlis*
Miss	*Homelia super "Missus est" in laudibus Virginis Matris*
Mor	*Epistola de moribus et officiis episcoporum*
Nat	*Sermo in nativitate Domini*
I Nov	*Sermo in dominica I novembris*
O Pasc	*Sermo in octava paschae*
Par	*Parabola*
Pent	*Sermo in die pentecostes*
PP	*Sermo in festo ss. apostolorum Petri et Pauli*
Pre	*De precepto et dispensatione*
QH	*Sermo super psalmum "Qui habitat"*
Res	*Sermo in resurrectione*
SC	*Sermo super Cantica canticorum*
I, II, or III Sent	*Sententia* (series prima, series secunda, series tertia)
S Mal	*Sermo de sancto Malachia*
Tpl	*Ad milites Templi de laude novae militiae*
Vict	*Sermo in natali sancti Victoris*
V Mal	*Vita sancti Malachiae*
V Nat	*Sermo in vigilia nativitatis Domini*

Biblical Abbreviations

Ac	Acts
Bar	Baruch
1 Chr	1 Chronicles
2 Chr	2 Chronicles
Col	Colossians
1 Cor	1 Corinthians
2 Cor	2 Corinthians
Dn	Daniel
Dt	Deuteronomy
Eph	Ephesians
Ex	Exodus
Ez	Ezekiel
Ezr	Ezra
Gal	Galatians
Gn	Genesis
Heb	Hebrews
Hos	Hosea
Is	Isaiah
Jas	James
Jb	Job
Jdt	Judith
Jer	Jeremiah
Jgs	Judges
Jl	Joel
Jn	John
1 Jn	1 John

Jon	Jonah
Jos	Joshua
Jr	Jeremiah
1 K	1 Kings
2 K	2 Kings
Lam	Lamentations
Lk	Luke
1 M	1 Maccabees
2 M	2 Maccabees
Mal	Malachi
Mi	Micah
Mk	Mark
Mt	Matthew
Nm	Numbers
Phil	Philippians
Prv	Proverbs
Ps	Psalm
1 Pt	1 Peter
Qo	Ecclesiastes; Qoheleth
Rom	Romans
Rv	Revelation
Sg	Song of Songs
Si	Ecclesiasticus; Sirach
1 Sm	1 Samuel
Tb	Tobit
1 Thes	1 Thessalonians
2 Thes	2 Thessalonians

Preface

On many occasions, I have tried to interpret Bernard for his spiritual daughters and sons living in Cistercian monasteries in Europe and America. On one such occasion, speaking to the monks of Holy Cross Abbey in Virginia, I tried to convince my audience that Bernard viewed monasticism as intrinsically superior to all other ways and states of life. One member of my audience, Brother James Sommers, objected strongly to the whole notion of a hierarchy of vocations. He protested that his friend, who had spent his life in the soup kitchens of Washington, D.C.'s slums, was leading a more holy life than he. I had written—and would write—a number of articles that I thought would refute Brother James's assertion. The clumsiness of my response to him did not shake my conviction—until many years later when I finally saw the full implications of Bernard's anthropology. The result is apparent in this volume. I am grateful to Brother James, and I should be grateful to all who correct the clumsy misinterpretations which I may make in this work.

My indebtedness is deep to Brother James and all his sisters and brothers who live in Cistercian monasteries. They have listened to me and corrected me—while providing me an experience of the life Bernard loved. I am indebted too to many generations of students at Western Michigan University, Michigan State University, and the University of Dallas. They have read Bernard and the other Cistercian authors with me. They have listened to my readings with critical ears and forced me to make my interpretations more coherent. They have also offered insights I should not otherwise have seen.

Translating Bernard's splendid Latin is a problem. I have consulted recent translations, and I have indicated their location in each footnote. But I have translated each quotation afresh—though I am more indebted to the translations in the Cistercian Fathers series than to others. The reader who consults Bruno Scott James's translation of Bernard's letters (*The Letters of St. Bernard of Clairvaux*, published by Burns Oates in 1953 and reprinted by Cistercian Publications in 1998) should know that James's numbering system does not correspond to that of the critical edition (SBOp).

Another potential source of confusion is the numbering of the Psalms in this volume. Bernard used the Vulgate text of the Bible, and I have followed him in this. Through Psalm 8, the numbering is the same as in the King James, Revised Standard, and other Protestant versions—as well as in the newer Catholic editions. From Psalm 10 to 112, one should add one number to those given. The Vulgate Psalm 113 is contained in Psalms 114 and 115 of the newer versions. The Vulgate 114–115 become 116; 116–145 become 117–146. Psalms 146 and 147 of the Vulgate version are contained in Psalm 147—and the rest have the same numbering.

I am profoundly grateful to Cathy Carol. She successfully undertook the onerous burden of preparing the typescript for the many permutations that this book has seen. I am also grateful to the scholar and gentleman who is the editor of this volume, Dr. Christopher Bellitto. The title of this work contains a grateful imitation of a phrase, "the spirituality of relationship," often heard from the ambo of the Church of the Incarnation at the University of Dallas. I have learned the phrase, and much of what it means, from Monsignor Milam Joseph, a wise and learned priest and prophet and for many happy years the president of the University.

I cannot adequately express my gratitude to my wife Patricia for the support and sacrifice that have made this volume possible. She joins me in thanksgiving for the long, deeply rewarding relationship we have enjoyed with Paschal Phillips, our dearest friend.

John R. Sommerfeldt
University of Dallas

1

Bernard, Society, and the Church

A. BERNARD IN THE SOCIETY OF HIS TIME

Bernard of Clairvaux was surely one of the most important leaders of Christendom in the first half of the twelfth century. Indeed, it could be argued that, in the later years of his life, Bernard was the most influential person in Europe. Bernard's role in the papal schism of 1130 and his preaching of the Second Crusade in 1146 provide significant evidence of that leadership.

According to one contemporary author, Arnold of Bonneval, Bernard single-handedly settled the papal schism at the request of the French bishops assembled at the Council of Étampes.[1] One must exercise some caution in accepting Arnold's interpretation, since others present at the council do not ascribe the same degree of influence to Bernard.[2] Nevertheless, it is clear that Bernard played a central and critical role in the acceptance of that council's decision for Innocent II. Bernard was untiring in his campaign, pursued successfully through letters,[3] travels, councils, and disputations. Martha Newman has written that Bernard's "letters and travels and the utter conviction with which he argued made . . . [his] position the dominant and, ultimately, the victorious one."[4] In an age in which religion is an important as it surely was in the twelfth century, the person instrumental in the choice of the head of the institutional expression of that religion is a person of great power. And from 1130 to his death in 1153, Bernard did not cease to play a role of primary significance in the affairs of his world.[5]

Bernard's role in preaching the Second Crusade was critical to the launching of that expedition.[6] His influence aroused the European conscience to the point that he could write to Pope Eugenius:

> You have commanded, and I have obeyed. And the authority of your command has made my obedience fruitful. Since "I have announced and have spoken, [the soldiers of the Cross] have increased beyond number [Ps 39:6]." Cities and castles are emptied, and now seven women can hardly find one man to hold [see Is 4:1]—so much so that everywhere there are widows whose husbands are still alive.[7]

In the course of launching the crusade, Bernard enrolled, at Vézelay in March 1146, the hosts of a willing—indeed, eager—King Louis VII of France.[8] At Speyer in December of 1146, Bernard enlisted the army of a hesitant emperor-elect Conrad III.[9] Conrad was understandably reluctant, since the tensions in Germany between his family, the Hohenstaufen, and the supporters of Conrad's old enemy, Duke Welf VI, approached a state of civil war. Bernard's influence, apparently aided by that of his Cistercian confrère, Abbot Adam of Ebrach, won Welf to the same cause as his ruler and thus enabled both sides to join in the crusading pilgrimage.[10] Due in large part to Bernard's efforts, a vast army of men took the cross and set out for the East.[11]

Bernard surely had a strong voice in the direction of the society of his time through his influence on the regularly constituted leaders of that society. Bernard was the preceptor of popes and the conscience of kings. Many of the over five hundred letters collected by Jean Leclercq[12] are addressed to popes, patriarchs, cardinals, archbishops, bishops, abbots, canons, and other clergy—exhorting them to fulfill their ministry according to the pattern of Christian virtue. Bernard admonished and praised lay leaders as well; he did not hesitate to write or preach to emperors, kings, and princes as the occasion seemed to demand. The administration of early twelfth-century society was thus subject to Bernard's surveillance. But that was not all.

Bernard also powerfully influenced significant aspects of the intellectual and spiritual life of Europe. Much scholarly labor has demonstrated Bernard's great contribution to contemporary theology and his influence on its development.[13] A telling index to Bernard's influence on intellectual and spiritual life is the number of manuscripts of his works that circulated throughout Europe during his own lifetime. And, as Jean Leclercq has written, "more than 1,500 manuscripts of Bernard's works have survived all threats of disappearance, and nearly half of these date from his own time. This high figure seems to constitute a unique case in literary history."[14] In short, Bernard was a leader in so many aspects of early twelfth-century culture that it is impossible to examine his age without studying him.

Bernard's leadership leads one to ask: How is it that a monk could play such a role? How is it that a man dedicated to withdrawal from the world could have so much influence on the world? My conviction is that Bernard could lead Europe to a crusade, powerfully influence who Europe's leaders were to be and how they were to act, and help shape the spiritual life of its inhabitants because his life embodied so many ideals of his age, some of which had not crystallized until his coming. The ideals of early twelfth-century Europe were largely unified around spiritual values. Thus it was possible for one man, who as a monk embodied those ideals most perfectly—it was thought—to give expression to the values of his age. Because of his genius, Bernard was able to explicate forcefully the ideals and values implicit in his society's choice of him as its leader. Jean Leclercq again:

> St. Bernard kept his finger on the pulse of his age and was therefore in real communion with it. This allowed him to express its deepest aspirations and conflicts in language movingly human yet symbolically divine. His words lifted men's hearts to long for God, to hunger for his compassionate and liberating love. Was it any wonder that he should, as a person, have had such great and ennobling influence not only on his monastic foundations but also on his own immediate surroundings and on secular society as a whole?[15]

B. Bernard on the Church

For Bernard, Church and society are two sides of the same coin, since he sees each person and group in society in terms of their place and role in the pilgrimage procession that has individual and corporate perfection as its goal.[16] Bernard is sure that society, that Church, is called to union with God, and thus all within Church and society are so called: "He [the Bridegroom] says: 'Arise, make haste my love, my dove, my beautiful one [Sg 2:10].' These words are not so applied to the Church as to exclude any one of us, who together are the Church, from a share in her blessings. For in this respect we are all, universally and without distinction, called to possess those blessings as our heritage [1 Pt 3:9]."[17] Bernard is convinced that "all the elect are what the Church is."[18] Even those who now live recklessly, ignoring their goal of perfection, must be considered part of the Church, must be "called daughters of Jerusalem."[19] The Church, then, "is the sum total of those for whom God is seeking in love and wishes to save . . . ."[20] The Church is for Bernard not merely an institution or a corporation. She is the sum total of all those pursuing, however feebly, the path to perfection.

The many images of Church that Bernard employs show his conviction that communal and individual happiness are intimately associated. Perhaps the most enduring image of Church in Bernard's works is that of bride, for "the Bridegroom of the Church [is] Jesus Christ, our Lord . . . ."[21] It is love that unites the Bridegroom to the bride, and Bernard claims he has "only one desire: . . . to show forth the hidden delights [of the love] between Christ and the Church."[22] That love relationship was born on the Cross: "From the heart of the Lord while he hung lifeless on the Cross 'there came out blood and water [Jn 19:34].' So that from the side of the new Adam, as he slumbered in death, might be produced and, at the same time, be redeemed the new Eve, the Church."[23] And because we are the Church, Bernard believes, "the Bridegroom is our God [see Ps 47:15], and we . . . are the bride—we and the whole multitude . . . whom he acknowledges."[24] Christ's bride is thus the whole "congregation of the righteous,"[25] and all become brides of Christ within the

one bride who is the Church.[26] Within the Church-bride all participate in the process of becoming brides.[27]

The same relationship of individual and community is evident in
Bernard's image of Church as mother:

> When the nurslings of the Church have fed from the breasts
> of wisdom and have tasted the sweetness of a better milk,
> already growing in grace, already satisfied with what they
> have received, they will say from the bottom of their heart:
> "The milk from your breasts is better than wine; the fra-
> grance of rare perfumes cannot match it for delight [Sg
> 1:1–2]." And this is what they say to their mother [the
> Church].[28]

That relationship is also explicit in Bernard's agricultural images of
the Church. Bernard is particularly fond of describing her as "the
vineyard of the Lord—that one, I mean, which encompasses the
world, of which we are a part—a vine great beyond measure, planted
by the Lord [see Ps 79:16], bought with his blood, fertilized by
grace, and made fruitful by his Spirit [see 1 Cor 3:6]."[29]

Bernard also employs images of the Church as city, as the new
Jerusalem, and as the body of Christ, in which all are members of
one another: ". . . Just as all things are in common in the [heavenly]
city [of Jerusalem; see Ps 121:3], so ought we to think [see Rom
12:16] and speak alike and have no divisions among us [see 1 Cor
1:10], but rather show that we are all one body [see 1 Cor 10:17]."[30]
The Church is a "city because [she is] an assembly of souls, a bride
because beloved, a sheep because gentle."[31]

It is in the image of the Church as the body of Christ that
Bernard reveals his own role in the Church. In writing to the citizens
of Rome standing in rebellion against their bishop, Bernard com-
pares the pope to the head of the body, the Church, and himself to
the tongue that speaks for that body:

> The trouble is in the head, and for this reason there is no
> member of the body so small or insignificant as not to be

affected by it, not even myself. This great trouble affects even me, although I am the least of all, because what affects the head cannot but affect the body of which I am a member. When the head is suffering, does not the tongue cry out for all the members of the body that the head is in pain, and do not all the members of the body confess by means of the tongue that the head is theirs and the pain too?[32]

I am convinced that this image contains an accurate description of Bernard's role in the early twelfth-century Church and in the society of the time. Bernard could be the tongue of his time because his penetrating analysis of the anatomy of that contemporary social body enabled him to express so well the ideals and values of his society.

C. The Three Orders in the Church

Although Bernard sees the Church as body, bride, city, vineyard, and sheepfold, he requires a more dynamic image to describe the life of the Church, for that life is a process, a process which, he believes, leads to perfection and is, at the same time, that perfection.[33] The image that Bernard employs is the sea, and the life of humans is a crossing of the sea. But that sea is crossed by more than one means and by more than one sort of person: "My brothers, this extensive sea [see Ps 103:25]...is traversed by three classes of persons, each crossing safely in its own way—so that they may pass over in deliverance [see Is 51:10]. The three are [typified by] Noah, Daniel, and Job [see Ez 14:14], of whom the first crossed by ship, the second by a bridge, the third by a ford."[34] Bernard sees Noah, Daniel, and Job signifying "the three orders of the Church":

Noah guided the ark, in which I perceive immediately the form of the Church of the just, so that it did not perish in the flood [see Gn 7:7]. Daniel, a man of longings [see Dn 9:23], dedicated himself to abstinence and chastity [see Dn 1:8]; this is the order of penance and continence which free one for

God alone. Job, too, dispensing well the goods of this world
[see Jb 1:3; 1 Jn 3:17] in the married state, signifies the faithful [laity] rightly possessing the goods of this world.[35]

Bernard identifies the three sorts of wayfarers as the continent, the
prelates, and married folk. Daniels are ". . . those who, holding back
from carnal attachments, are converted to attachments of the heart
[see Ps 84:9], to spiritual desires, which is why Daniel was called a
man of desires by the angel [see Dn 10:11]." Noahs are the prelates
who "apply themselves more to profit others than to ruling over
them [see RB 64], for holiness is greatly becoming to them [see Ps
92:5], which is why they are called 'saints' in the psalm [see Ps
84:9]." "Then," says Bernard, "there are the married folk, who do
not transgress the commandments, so that they may be called justly
the people of God [see Ps 84:9] and the sheep of his pasture [see Ps
94:7]."[36]

The three orders have much in common. They are all in need of
God's mercy,[37] but they are also all capable of producing heroes of
the faith, those who respond to God's mercy in an exemplary way.[38]
The heroic virtues of martyrdom are not demanded of all, but all are
called to fervor in the faith. "This," Bernard says, "is a common
obligation; this is required of everyone."[39]

If fervor is a virtue that should be common to all, all orders are
equally subject to temptation to hypocrisy. Bernard writes: "The hyp-
ocrite sees himself engaged in a great and honorable business. Clev-
erly and skillfully he sells piecemeal what he has of good conscience
for a mean price, be it for praise or for some similar reward. This business is carried out in the darkness, in the hiddenness of pretense. It is
said to prowl [see Ps 90:6] because no rank or order or person escapes
this temptation."[40] But Bernard's response to this threat is characteris-
tically optimistic: to counter the universal temptation to self-deception,
to dishonesty with oneself and others, God's gift of wisdom can be
had by all simply for the asking. Bernard prays: "The fragrance of your
wisdom comes to us in what we hear, for, if anyone needs wisdom, let
that one but ask for wisdom and you will give it to him or her [see Jas
1:5]. It is well known that you give to all freely and ungrudgingly."[41]

Bernard's enthusiasm for all orders in Church and society is matched by his confidence in their response to God's invitation to perfection and in the power to attain happiness, which he believes God freely bestows.

Whatever order in society to which one belongs or whatever spiritual mode one finds most compatible with one's nature and needs, Bernard is confident that balance and integration are found in the community that is the Church: "Which of us can live uprightly and perfectly even for one hour, an hour free from fruitless talk and careless work? Yet there is one who truthfully and unhesitatingly can glory in this praise. She is the Church, whose fullness is a never-ceasing font of intoxicating joy, perpetually fragrant."[42] The fullness that informs the Church is her possession of the virtues of all, for

> what she lacks in one member she possesses in another, according to the measure of Christ's gift [see Eph 4:7] and the plan of the Spirit who distributes to each one just as he chooses [see 1 Cor 12:11]. The Church's fragrance is radiated by those who use their money... to win themselves friends [see Lk 16:9]. She intoxicates by the words of her preachers, who drench the earth and make it drunk [see Ps 64:10] with the wine of spiritual gladness and yield a harvest through their perseverance [see Lk 8:15].[43]

Rejoicing in her own intoxicating fragrance, the Church makes bold to claim once more the title and role of bride:

> With the bold assurance of one confident that her breasts are better than wine and redolent of the choicest perfumes [see Sg 1:1–3], she lays claim to the title of bride. Although none of us would dare arrogate the title of the Lord's bride to his or her own soul, nevertheless we are members of the Church who rightly boasts of this title and of the reality that it signifies, and hence we may justifiably assume a share in this honor. For what all of us together possess in a full and perfect manner, that each single one of us undoubtedly possesses by participation.[44]

Bernard responds to this participation in perfection with gratitude for the gift that enables each individual to play the role of Christ's bride "in an embrace that is sweet, chaste, and eternal, beholding with unveiled face [see 2 Cor 3:18] that glory which is...[his] in union with the Father and the Holy Spirit for ever and ever."[45]

Bernard's gratitude to God, he thinks, is well deserved. The riches of perfection God gives not merely to a select few, but are available to all folk. Bernard sees the heretics of his time "cutting Christ off from all kinds of people of both sexes, young and old, living and dead":

> They put infants outside the sphere of grace because they are too young to receive it, and those who are full grown because they find difficulty in preserving chastity. They deprive the dead of the help of the living and rob the living of the prayers of the saints because they have died. God forbid! The Lord will not forsake his people [see 1 K 12:22] who are as the sands of the sea [see Gn 32:12], nor will he who redeemed all be content with a few, and those heretics. For his redemptive gift is not a trifling thing; it is extremely abundant [see Ps 129:7].[46]

And God's redemptive gift takes many forms, each form appropriate to the needs of the recipient:

> Thus, just as the soul sees with her eyes, hears with her ears, smells with her nose, tastes with her mouth, touches with the rest of her body, so God accomplishes different ends through different spirits. For example, in some he shows himself loving, in others perceiving, in still others doing other things— just as the manifestation of the Spirit is given to each for his or her own good [see 1 Cor 12:7].[47]

Unity in diversity is a fundamental motif recurring throughout Bernard's teaching on Church and society. His *Apology to Abbot William*[48] offers some important observations on the orders of the Church, once again symbolized by the wayfarers Noah, Daniel, and

Job. If the variance between the lifestyles of these wayfarers were in opposition, he asserts,

> by the same reasoning...we should have to think that celibates and married folk condemn each other because they live according to their own laws within the Church. Monks and regular clerics would be said to derogate one another because their observances separate one from another. We should never suspect that Noah, Daniel, and Job [see Ez 14:14] each have a share in the one kingdom because we perceive that they do not follow the same path of justice. Then Mary and Martha, one or the other, must have displeased their Savior, since their efforts to please him were so very unlike [see Lk 10:38–42]. By this reasoning there could be neither peace nor harmony in all the Church—a Church, as we read in the Psalm [44:15], arrayed like a queen in variety, with many and dissimilar orders.[49]

The different orders of society are united in one many-colored robe, a robe "famous for its many colors, distinctive in its most beautiful variety [see Gn 37:3]."[50] Bernard prays to the Father that he might more fully "recognize the many-colored robe you have made for your Anointed. Some folk you have set aside as apostles, others as prophets. Some are preachers, others are pastors and teachers or fulfill some other role [see 1 Cor 12:28] in the wondrous decoration of this garment. All contribute to the consummation of the saints; all run toward human perfection according to the measure of Christ's fullness [see Eph 4:12–13]."[51] Joseph's robe, which is the many-colored, seamless robe of the Christ, is Jesus' gift to the Church. This robe "is many-colored because of the many orders, distinct in many ways, which exist within it. It is seamless because of the undivided unity of indissoluble love."[52] Thus, Bernard concludes,

> there must be no division within the Church. She must remain whole and integral according to her inherited right. For about her it has been written: "At your right hand stands the queen in a golden robe, surrounded with variety [Ps 44:10]." This is

why different people receive different gifts [see 1 Cor 7:7].
One receives one kind, one another, whether a Cluniac or a
Cistercian [monk], whether a regular cleric or one of the faithful laity. This applies to every order, to every language, to both
sexes, to every age, to every condition, in all places, through
all time, from the first person down to the last. . . . Let us work
together to form a single robe, and let this one robe include us
all.[53]

Bernard senses how beneficial this variety is to all the folk who
participate in the unity of the Church despite the diversity of their
lifestyles: "It may be asked me why, since I praise all orders, I do not
hold to all. For I do praise and love all, wherever in the Church one
lives piously and justly. I hold to one by my work, to the others by
my love. Yet I trust that my love will bring it about that I shall share
in the fruits of those orders to which I do not belong."[54] This diversity in the Church, Bernard holds, is appropriate to a community on
pilgrimage to its ultimate destination. Even in the house of the Lord
to which that community journeys there will be diversity, a diversity
that injures neither unity nor equality:

... It is written: "In my Father's house there are many rooms
[Jn 14:2]." Just as there are many rooms in one house there,
so here there are many orders in one Church. Just as on
earth there are different gifts but the one Spirit [see 1 Cor
12:4], so in heaven there are different types of glory within a
single house. Here as there, unity consists in one love. Here
diversity consists in the division of the orders and their many
tasks [see 1 Cor 12:6]; there diversity will consist of an obvious and well-ordered distinction of merits. The Church
understands that there is within herself at once a concordant
discord and a discordant concord . . . .[55]

The discordant concord sounding within and throughout the Church
is a product of God's loving care and direction, for God "appointed
some in the Church to be apostles, some prophets, others evange-
lists, others pastors and teachers, for the perfecting of the saints [see

Eph 4:11]."[56] The proper response to God's ordering of the Church in love is an echoing human love. Bernard is confident that this loving response to love will lead each person to his or her goal of happiness, no matter what order to which he or she belongs, no matter what path he or she follows; for "there is not just one path to follow, just as there is not only one [heavenly] room toward which we journey. One should look to the path one follows and not be so concerned with alternate paths that one deviates from the one justice [which informs all]. For whatever path one follows to whatever [heavenly] room, no one will be left outside the Father's house."[57]

11
The Monastic Order of Daniel

The path to perfection that Bernard himself follows is, of course, that of the monk.[1] His path is the way of Daniel, the man of longings. Daniel crossed the waters of life by means of a bridge;[2] over this bridge all monks can run with confidence. "The bridge," Bernard says, "is constructed of three kinds of wood upon which we can put our whole weight without our foot slipping. The woods are bodily hardship, poverty in the goods of the world, and the humility of obedience."[3] Continuing his exercise in monastic carpentry, Bernard declares: "The woods must be properly put together. For bodily hardship cannot be easily maintained among riches or discreetly practiced without obedience. Poverty cannot exist for a single moment amidst pleasure and self-will, and obedience amidst riches and pleasure is neither stable nor glorious."[4] Monks of every kind run over this bridge, on a path both glorious and hidden.[5]

A. THE PARADISE OF THE CLOISTER

Bernard is a monk, and his joy in his monastic profession is infectious, indeed contagious:

> Dear brothers, you are walking in the way that leads to life [see Mt 7:14], in the way, direct and undefiled, which leads to the holy city of Jerusalem [see Dn 3:28] which is free, which is above, which is our mother [see Gal 4:26]. The ascent is difficult, since this road runs straight up to the summit of the

mountain. But this hard way is shorter in length, both well laid out and remote. But you not only walk, you run up it with happy ease and easy happiness, for you are girded for the journey and carry no burdens on your backs.[6]

Bernard's joy in the life of the monk is the result of his conviction that in it one follows the counsel of Christ to "sell what you have . . . and come follow me."[7]

It is at Clairvaux that Bernard feels the greatest joy in his calling. He shares that joy with Alexander, the bishop of Lincoln, in describing the new life at Clairvaux that Alexander's friend Philip has embraced while on the way to the Holy Land:

> I write to tell you that your Philip has found a short cut to Jerusalem and has arrived there very quickly. . . . He is . . . a devout inhabitant and enrolled citizen of Jerusalem—not of that earthly Jerusalem to which Mount Sinai in Arabia is joined, which is in bondage with her children, but of that free Jerusalem which is above and is our mother [Gal 4:25–26]. And this, if you wish to know, is Clairvaux. She is the Jerusalem united to the one in heaven by whole-hearted devotion, by imitation of life, by a certain spirit of kinship. Here Philip takes his rest, as he has promised, for ever and ever [see Ps 131:14]. He has chosen Clairvaux as his dwelling [see Ps 131:13] because within her he has found, not yet the vision, but surely the expectation of true peace, "the peace of God which is so much greater than we can understand [Phil 4:7]."[8]

Clairvaux and, indeed, all genuine monasteries are Jerusalems, for "the cloister is a true paradise, a region protected by the wall of discipline, in which is fecund fertility of the most precious goods. It is a glorious thing when men of one way of life dwell in a house [see Ps 67:7]. How good and pleasant it is for brethren to dwell together in unity [see Ps 132:1]!"[9] That unity is all the more precious because of the diversity of the ministries of the men within the monastery:

There you will see one weeping over his sins, another rejoicing in the praises of God, this one ministering to all, that one teaching others. You will see one praying, another engaged in meditative reading, this one commiserating, that one correcting. You will see one inflamed with love, another mighty with humility, this one humble in prosperity, that one sublime in adversity. You will see one assiduous in action, another quiet in contemplation. And you will be able to say: "These are the camps of God [Gn 32:2]."[10]

The paradise of the cloister is also a marketplace. Within it, the monk is a merchant who carries on a business venture that reaps high rewards. In Bernard's seventh *Parable,* he offers this exchange: "'...Tell me, O great trader,' [the Lord says,] 'where did you carry on your business? Where have you made these profits? Where have you gained all these things?' The monk [replies]: 'In the monastery. In the cloister....'"[11] Whether Bernard's image is sublime or mundane, his message is the same. Whether seen as a Jerusalem, a paradise, or a marketplace,[12] the monastery is the dwelling of those who follow Daniel across the sea of life by a secure bridge, by a safe path.

The invitation to enter Jerusalem, paradise, the marketplace, is open to all who would enter: "We in the monasteries accept all [sorts of] folk, with the hope of improving them."[13] And there they will find rest: "Within the Church, the bed [see Sg 1:15] where one reposes is, I believe, the cloisters and monasteries where one lives undisturbed by the cares of the world and the anxieties of life [see Lk 8:14, 21:34]."[14] But this rest from the cares of the world is not restfull. For within the cloister monks must struggle with the temptations and difficulties of their way of life.[15] The burdens that monks must bear on their path to perfection may be heavy, but their way will be eased by identification with Christ and by his consolation:

Do not let the roughness of our life frighten your tender years....If the sweetness of Christ is present, the inedible meal of the Prophet [see 2 K 4:41] will be savored with sauce. If you feel the sting of temptation, look upon the bronze serpent raised on the staff [see Nm 21:8–9] and drink not only from the wounds but from the breasts of the Crucified. For he will be a mother to you and you a son to him. Joined to the Crucified, the nails which pierce his and your hands and feet cannot injure too severely.[16]

The path of the monk is rough, but on it the monk follows the way of Christ. It is a sure path to perfection, a secure bridge over the sea of life.

B. Daniel's Virtues and Practices

Life within the monastery is vigorous but seemed to Bernard "so close to the ideal program for human existence that he unceasingly referred to it."[17] In a letter to the monks of Saint Jean d'Aulps, Bernard describes that life in terms of both practices and virtues: "Our place is at the bottom, is humility. Our place is voluntary poverty, obedience, and joy in the Holy Spirit. Our place is under a master, under an abbot, under a rule, under discipline. Our place is to cultivate silence and exert ourselves in fasts, vigils, prayers, manual labor. And, above all, our place is to keep that 'more excellent way [1 Cor 12:31]' which is the way of love."[18] A disciplined life thus leads the monk from humility to love. These are the fundamental virtues of the good life, as Bernard sees it.[19] Thus the monastery is an institution structured to foster the virtues common to all Christians, to all humans.

Monastic life is an integrated life in which every activity is directed toward promoting virtue. And in these activities the monks are united in fraternal love. Though parted from his monks temporarily, Bernard writes his sons and brothers: "Whoever among you shows himself ready to serve, humble, reverent, zealous in meditative reading, attentive in prayer, solicitous of fraternal love, can be sure I am not absent from him."[20] Bernard is more specific about monastic practices in describing the temptations placed before his monk and nephew Ralph to lure him away from Clairvaux: "He [the tempter] preempts, he allures, he coaxes, and this preacher of a new gospel commends intoxication and condemns fasting. He says that voluntary poverty is irksome; he calls fasting, vigils, silence, and manual labor insanity. On the other hand, sloth he pronounces contemplation; gluttony, loquacity, curiosity, and all intemperance he calls discretion....What sort of religion, [he asks,] is it to dig the soil, clear forests, and cart dung?"[21] Bernard is sure that the dung cart carries the monk to the bed of the Bridegroom. He has the monk-become-bride say:

> Do you not see that, by his grace, I have been careful—for many years now—to lead a chaste and sober life [see Ti 2:12]. I persist in meditative reading; I resist vices. I apply myself frequently to prayer; I am watchful against temptations; I think over my past in the bitterness of my soul [see Is 38:15]. As far as I can judge, I have lived among the brethren without quarrel [see Phil 3:6]. I have been submissive to authority [see Ti 3:1], going out and coming back at the command of my senior. I do not covet the goods of others; rather I put myself and my goods at the service of others. In the sweat of my brow I eat my bread [see Gn 3:19].[22]

Physical labor and meditative reading, activities of both body and mind, are equal components of the life of virtue as lived in a monastery.

The monk is pledged to stability within his family, to obedience to that family and its father, and, within it, to convert his way of life, that is, to turn his will toward God. Following the *Rule* of Benedict of Nursia, the monk "must promise in the oratory, in the presence of all, stability, conversion of life, and obedience."[23] Bernard puts these vows into the context of the whole monastic life in assuring the monks of Flay that their brother, who left Flay for Clairvaux, is living as a good monk: "I bear witness that he never wanders abroad, but, peacefully persevering in the monastery, he lives without quarrel the life of a poor man among the poor. Far from having betrayed the faith he first pledged with you, he now ratifies it. Together with obedience and conversion of life, without which he is deceived who trusts in his stability of place, he now keeps that faith whole and entire."[24]

The monastic vows are properly lived in a context of simplicity. Bernard is certain that simplicity is the path that leads to Christ and his love: "...I know that many of you walk in the love with which

Christ has loved us [see Eph 5:2] and seek him in simplicity of heart [see Ws 1:1]."[25] Simplicity is expressed in cheap, but serviceable clothing,[26] and in straightforward, unadorned architecture[27] and undistracting liturgy.[28] Simplicity conveys an honesty that rejects duplicity and deception; it avoids all that could confuse the monk in his quest for love and happiness. "Be simple with your Lord," Bernard advises, "putting away not only all guile and simulation, but equally all multiplicity of occupation, so that you may converse freely with him whose voice is so sweet and face so comely [see Sg 2:14]."[29] The simple physical environment and honest activities of the monk promote in him virtues that liberate him for a life of love.

This is why the monk pledges his stability, obedience, and conversion of life in a family dedicated to a common aspiration: ". . . Live simply," Bernard says, "among your brethren, seeking God, submissive to your superior, obedient to your seniors, friendly to your juniors, pleasing the angels, profitable in speech, humble of heart, kind to all."[30] Obedience, then, is an expression of love, not subservience. Bernard admonishes his monks: ". . . 'Be eager always to preserve unity in the bonds of peace, exhibiting toward all,' but especially toward your superiors, 'the humble love which is the bond of perfection [1 Pt 4:8].'"[31] Stability is attachment to a loving family, a family open to the Spirit and united in love of Christ: "Let us pray, brothers, that . . . the Holy Spirit may always find us all in the same place [see Ac 2:1] not only by bodily presence because of our promised stability, but also by unity of hearts."[32]

Living in a family informed by love, the monk spends his time not only in the prayer implied by his profession,[33] but in the multitude of practical, down-to-earth activities necessary to the life of the household of God.[34] Bernard finds an appropriate image of that household in the family of Martha, Mary, and Lazarus. Bernard sees ". . . Martha as serving, Mary in repose, and Lazarus as groaning beneath the stone, beseeching the gift of resurrection [see Jn 11:39–44]."[35] The roles of all three are to be combined in the monk's life: "Each one will be counted perfect in whom their three endowments are united in due order and degree, so that he will know how to mourn his sins and rejoice in God, and at the same time assist his neighbors. He will please God, watch out for himself, and be of service to his friends."[36]

"But," Bernard asks, "who is up to all of these?" The solution to this dilemma is the specialization of function already present in the structure of the monastic household:

> Please God...[these practices] may be preserved down the years among us all, if not all three in each one, at least singly in different persons. For we discover Martha as the Savior's friend in those who do the daily chores. We find Lazarus, the mourning dove [see Is 59:11], in the novices newly dead to their sins [see 1 Pt 2:24], who toil with fresh wounds and mourn through fear of judgment. . . . We find a contemplative Mary in those who, cooperating with God's grace over a long period of time, have attained to a better and happier state. By now confident of forgiveness, they no longer brood anxiously on the sad memory of their sins. But day and night they meditate on the ways of God with insatiable delight [see Ps 1:2]—even at times gazing with unveiled face [see 2 Cor 3:18], in unspeakable joy, on the splendor of the Bridegroom, being transformed into his likeness from splendor to splendor by the Spirit of the Lord.[37]

Although the monk's life necessarily entails embracing the contemplative life of Mary, he must also do Martha's part in the functioning of the family of God: "If you consider that the house in question is an earthly house, you will easily understand why it was Martha and not Mary who received the Lord into it."[38] Only when Martha finds herself insufficient to the task assigned should she seek to have her function assigned to another.[39]

But Martha should never be a busybody; Bernard presents a caricature of one such monk in his *Steps of Humility and Pride:*

> When a man thinks he is better than others, will he not put himself before others? He must have the first place in gatherings, be the first to speak in council. He comes without being called. He interferes without being asked. He must rearrange everything, redo whatever has been done. What he himself did not do or arrange is not rightly done or properly

arranged. He is the judge of all judges and decides every case beforehand. If he is not made prior [see RB 65] when a vacancy occurs, he knows that the abbot is jealous of him or has been deceived. If obedience calls him to some ordinary tasks, he refuses disdainfully. A man fitted for higher positions could not be occupied with lesser things.[40]

To balance this fictional picture of the monk gone wrong, Bernard offers the reality of Gerard, his brother by birth and brother within the monastic family at Clairvaux. In his funeral oration for Gerard, Bernard tells us that he was both a Martha and a Mary, a man of deep spiritual power and insight:

> Spiritual men who knew him knew that his words bore a spiritual aroma. His comrades knew that his dispositions and propensities were anything but worldly [see Rom 8:5]; they were alive with spiritual power [see Rom 12:11]. Who was more uncompromising than he in the maintenance of discipline? Who was more austere in restraining bodily impulses, more absorbed in contemplation, more skilled in discussion? How often when talking with him have I increased my knowledge—I who approached him to enlighten him came away enlightened instead![41]

But this man of Mary's sort was also of Martha's kind, and his "skilled eye" was capable of supervising all the physical activities within the monastery.[42] This is Bernard's ideal monk, one who follows both Mary's and Martha's path to friendship with Christ and, Bernard is convinced, to the complete fulfillment of union with his Friend.

C. The Abbot as Prelate

Gerard, Bernard's brother by blood and in religion, saved him many a distraction from his abbatial role of teaching and provided him the quiet needed to serve his brothers in that role. Bernard tells us that he left me little more than the name and honor of provider; he did all the work. I was saluted as abbot, but he was the one who watched over all with solicitude [see Rom 12:8]. I could not but feel secure with a man who enabled me to enjoy the delights of divine love [see Ps 36:4], to preach unimpeded, to pray untroubled. I repeat that you, my brother, brought me a peaceful mind and a welcome peace. Through you my preaching was more effective, my prayer more fruitful, my meditative reading more frequent, and my love more fervent.[43]

Bernard's abbot and Bernard as abbot have responsibilities that go beyond that of the ordinary monk.

These responsibilities mean that the abbot is not only a Daniel but also a Noah. Addressing abbots and monks, Bernard tells them: "I propose to speak of the first and second orders [of prelates and of monks] because there are present my venerable brothers and fellow-abbots of the order of prelates, as well as monks of the order of penitence. However, we abbots may not think ourselves outside this second order, unless—God forbid—we are unmindful of our profession because of the office we hold."[44] The abbot, though elected a prelate, remains a monk.[45] His duties, however, are those of a prelate. The abbot ministers to the needs of those for whom he is responsible:

The prelate should possess a pure heart [see 1 Tm 1:5] if he desires to do good rather than merely rule. He must not seek his own interests or worldly honor—or any thing other than what is pleasing to God and serves the salvation of souls. But, with a pure intention and an irreproachable life, he must be a model for the flock [see 1 Pt 5:3] and begin to do and teach [see Ac 1:1]. As the *Rule* of our teacher [Benedict] enjoins: "By his deeds he must make it clear that nothing may be done which he has taught his disciples is forbidden [RB 2]." Otherwise, a brother whom he corrects may murmur quietly: "Physician, heal yourself [Lk 4:23]."[46]

The abbot must live for the welfare of his monks, for their happiness.[47]

The abbot must also be a model for his monks. He must be a teacher as well, ready with "useful teaching" for his sons.[48] But to preach and teach as he must, the abbot must also be a bride, a bride who receives the ecstatic embrace of the Bridegroom and thus begets and nurses her offspring:

> See how she [the bride] yearns for one thing and receives another. In spite of her longing for contemplation, she is burdened with the task of preaching. Despite her desire to bask in the Bridegroom's presence, she is entrusted with the cares of begetting and rearing children. Nor is this the only time she has been so treated. As you may remember, once before, when she had sighed for the Bridegroom's embrace and kiss, his response to her was: "Your breasts are better than wine [Sg 1:1]." And this made her realize that she was a mother, that her duty was to suckle her babes, to provide food for her children. . . . So now too, the bride, desiring and enquiring about the place where her beloved pastures his flock and rests at noon [see Sg 1:6], is given instead orna-ments of gold studded with silver [see Sg 1:10], wisdom with eloquence, and committed to the work of preaching.[49]

But preaching is not the only task of the abbot. He must act both as apostle and prophet, both in preaching and in providing guidance:

> I am neither prophet nor apostle, but, I must say, I act the role of both prophet and apostle. Though far beneath them in merit, I am caught up in similar cares. Even though it be a great embarrassment, though it puts me at serious risk, I am seated on the chair of Moses [see Mt 23:2], to whose quality of life I do not lay claim and whose gifts I do not experience. But, then, should one withhold respect for the chair because the one sitting there is unworthy?[50]

The tasks of preaching and guidance require spiritual maturity, the maturity of a bride and mother:

With the wisdom of Paul [in Rom 12:15], I shall assign these two affections to the bride's two breasts, compassion to one and congratulation to the other. She is but a girl too immature to marry and with breasts still underdeveloped if she is not prompted to congratulation, prone to condolence. If such a one should assume the governance of souls or the office of preaching, she would do no good for others and great harm to herself.[51]

In preaching and giving counsel to those entrusted to him, the abbot must exercise great discernment:

We must return to the breasts of the bride [see Sg 1:1] and show how both they and their milk differ. Congratulation yields the milk of encouragement, compassion that of consolation. As often as the spiritual mother receives the kiss [of the Bridegroom], she feels both breasts flowing with heavenly milk. You may see her nourishing her babes, suckling them with full breasts, from one the milk of consolation, from the other the milk of encouragement, according as she sees is the need of each.[52]

The abbot's wise discernment is especially needed in ascertaining motivation. Bernard writes to a nun seeking to leave her monastery for the eremetical life: "You would have done better to choose someone more learned than I to counsel you on this matter, but, as you have seen fit to do so, I shall not hide what seems better to me. I have thought and rethought the plan you have presented, but I do not dare to give an easy response. You could have zeal for God in mind, in which case your motivation is excusable . . . ."[53] But whether preaching or discerning or giving counsel, the abbot is always to keep in mind his service to those who need it most: "You must see yourself the abbot and father of those whom you find sad, faint-hearted, and discontented. It is by consoling, encouraging, and admonishing that you do your duty, that you bear your burden. And, by bearing that burden, you carry to health those who need healing."[54]

The burdens of the abbot are onerous indeed. Bernard's response to the burdens of counseling his brethren are mixed. He regrets the loss of leisure for meditation, but still feels impelled by love to spend himself on the needs of his monks:

> There are some sitting here [see Mt 16:28] whom I wish
> ...might begin to spare me a little bit more than in the past
> and not intrude rudely and irresponsibly on my leisure....I
> make this complaint reluctantly, however, for some timid
> persons might conceal their needs and overtax their powers
> of endurance through fear of disturbing me....They will
> spare me by not sparing me, and I shall rest more in knowing
> they are not afraid to trouble me about their needs. I shall
> accommodate myself to them as far as I can [see Ps 145:2].
> As long as I shall live I shall serve God in them, in unfeigned
> love [see 2 Cor 6:6].[55]

Responding to requests for guidance is burdensome, but Bernard is diligent in response.[56]

Preaching is a continuing burden, for "no small effort and fatigue are involved in going out day by day to draw waters from the open streams of the Scriptures and providing for the needs of each of you...."[57] The burden is great, for it is a distraction from the meditation in which Bernard finds his greatest joy. He exclaims: "How I wish that all had the gift of teaching! I should be rid of the need to preach these sermons! It is a burden I should like to transfer to another. Or, rather, I should prefer that none of you would need to exercise it and that all would be taught [directly] by God [see Jn 6:45]. Then I should have leisure to contemplate God's beauty [see Ps 45:11]."[58] Bernard also fears potential damage to his spiritual life by his assumption of the office of preacher; yet he must be of service to his monks: "If I spoke with profit about humility, I feared I might be found lacking in it. If humility kept me silent, I should be good for nothing."[59]

Bernard sees the conflict resolved in himself and, he counsels, in all abbots by an assessment of the motives behind both the leisure of meditation and the intense activity of preaching and guidance. Love must motivate both, and in that love, action and contemplation become one.[60] Bernard addresses the question through a speech of the bride of the Song of Songs to her bridesmaids: "She speaks to them this way: 'Be happy, be confident, "the king has brought me into his bedroom [Sg 1:3]."' You may view yourselves brought in too. Even though I alone seem to have been brought in, that is not for my advantage alone. Every gift I enjoy is a joy for you. And with you I shall divide all that I merit over your measure."[61] The love of the Bridegroom for the bride overflows to all through the preaching and guidance of the abbot. The abbot's leisure for meditation is the source of this service to his monks, and, like Paul, Bernard's abbot is compelled to share the fruits of his contemplation.[62] The bride, fresh from her bed of contemplative union with her Spouse, is sent out to bring forth fruit for him.[63] The willing and wholehearted response of the abbot must be to hasten away to serve his monks in love.

III

The Clerical Order of Noah

Like abbots, bishops[1] are the "prelates," who, as Noahs, steer the ark of the Church across the sea of life;[2] they are those "'who go down to the sea in ships, doing their work in the many waters [Ps 106:23].' They are not confined to one route, whether bridge or ford. They are thus free to move about in any direction and can meet the needs of all, as they are bound to do."[3] Using this freedom, prelates "guide their [people's] steps across bridge or ford; they direct those crossing. They discover and guard against dangers; they arouse the tepid and sustain the faint-hearted."[4]

The clergy are not only guides, they are physicians who "know that they have been chosen, not for the vain prestige of holding office, but to take care of ailing souls."[5] When these spiritual physicians "detect the presence of inner discontent from complaints—expressed even in insults or humiliating words—they must see themselves as physicians, not masters. And, rather than retaliate, they must prepare medicine for the fevered mind."[6] The prelates' guiding and healing ministry must be at once maternal and paternal. "Learn," Bernard admonishes, "that you must be mothers, not masters, to those in your care. Make an effort to arouse the response of love, not fear [see RB 64]. Should there be an occasional need for severity, let it be paternal, not tyrannical. Show affection as a mother; correct like a father. Be gentle, avoid harshness; do not resort to blows. Expose your breasts; let your breast swell with milk, not your bosom with passion."[7]

A. Images of the Clergy

The clergy are thus the fertile brides of the heavenly Bridegroom. They, "like holy mothers, bring souls to birth by their preaching...."[8] They nourish their offspring by "the breasts of preaching."[9] Bernard tells the clergy that, by the breasts they extend in preaching, "you deliver us from the selfish passions that attack the soul [see 1 Pt 2:11]; you snatch us from the world and gain us for God.... 'Your breasts are better than wine [Sg 1:1]'.... The spiritual delights that your breasts distill can conquer in us the pleasures of the flesh that have enslaved us just as drunkards are enslaved by wine."[10] The clergy are at once brides and friends of the Bridegroom, friends who deliver all to whom they minister into the arms of their Bridegroom.[11]

Bernard's imagery is as rich as his teaching. The clergy are public fountains from whom all may drink: "The fool and the wise man [see Qo 6:8], the slave and the freeman [see Eph 6:8], the rich and the poor man [see Prv 22:2], man and woman [see Gn 1:27], the old and the young [see Jer 31:13], cleric and layman, the just and the impious [see Gn 18:25] all share equally in you. They all drink from the public fountain of your breast...."[12] Wise clergy act not only as fountains; they also function as reservoirs: "The man who is wise... will see his life more like a reservoir than a canal. The canal pours out as it receives. The reservoir retains the water until it is filled, then discharges the overflow without loss to itself."[13] Bernard regrets that

> today there are many in the Church who act like canals; the reservoirs are far too rare. So urgent is the love of those through whom the streams of heavenly teaching flow to us that they wish to pour it forth before they have been filled. They are more ready to speak than to listen, impatient to teach what they have not grasped, and full of the presumption to govern others while they know not how to govern themselves.[14]

The clergy are not only dispensers of living waters, they also lead folk over the waters of life by the bridge that leads to God. A pontiff must himself be a *pons*, a bridge between his neighbor and God:[15]

This bridge reaches all the way to God in faithfulness, insofar as the pontiff seeks not his own glory but God's [see Jn 7:18]. And it extends to all in kindness, for the pontiff desires not his own advantage but his fellow-creatures'. As a true mediator, the pontiff offers God the prayers and sacrifices of the people and receives from him blessing and grace in return.... He is a faithful pontiff [see Heb 2:17], for everything that passes through his hands he views with the simple eyes of the dove. He keeps nothing for himself, whether God's gifts to his people or the gifts they bring to him. The pontiff seeks not the gifts but the salvation of his people, and he does not usurp the honor of God.[16]

Bernard's clergy are to be shepherds, pastors. He writes his former monastic son Eugenius, now bishop of Rome: "You must expel evil beasts from your boundaries so that your flocks may be led to pasture in safety. Banish the wolves, but do not lord it over the sheep. You have charge of them not to oppress but to feed them."[17] Bernard sees the clergy as part of a great company of shepherds who, from the time of the apostles, have tended the flock of God: "The only profit they sought from their sheep, their only glory, their only desire, was in some way to prepare them as perfect people for the Lord [see Lk 1:17]. They devoted every effort to this, even in great suffering of mind and body, in labor and hardship, in hunger and thirst, in cold and nakedness [see 2 Cor 11:27]."[18]

Bernard describes the clergy through horticultural and agricultural images as well. They are the gardeners of the Bridegroom who carefully cultivate and water the garden of the Church with their teaching.[19] A hearty image is provided by the picture Bernard paints of the cleric—in this case, the pope—as a sweating farmer at work:

Spiritual labor is well expressed by the image of the sweating farmer. And, therefore, we shall understand ourselves better if we realize that a ministry has been imposed on us rather than a dominion bestowed.... Learn by the example of the prophet to preside, not so much to command as to work at what the times require. Learn that you need a hoe, not a scepter, to do the work of the prophet. Indeed, he did not rise up to reign but to root out. Do you think you too can find work to be done in the fields of your Lord? Much indeed.[20]

The cleric is given power in order to perform his ministerial function in the fields of the Lord. But he must always remember that he is but a steward; the fields are his master's. Bernard writes Pope Eugenius III:

> Is not an estate made subject to a steward and a young lord to a teacher? Yet the steward is not lord of the estate, nor is the teacher lord of his lord. So, too, you should preside to provide, to counsel, to minister, to serve. Preside so as to be useful; preside so as to be the faithful and prudent servant whom the Lord has set up over his family [see Mt 24:45]. For what purpose? So you may give them food in due season, so you may minister, not rule.[21]

But, as hard as the cleric must labor in and over the fields of the Lord, he must acknowledge that the harvest is the Lord's, not his. Indeed, the laborer and steward must be content with no harvest at all. "Plant, water, take care," counsels Bernard, "and you will have done your duty. Do not fear; God, not you, will bring the grain to harvest in his own time [see 1 Cor 3:6–7]. Whenever he does not wish it, you will lose nothing. As Scripture says: 'God will reward the labors of his saints [Ws 10:17].' It is a labor which is truly without risk, which no failure can compromise."[22]

Bernard also employs the image of a city which is the Church to describe the clergy who watch over it all the "more diligently when they see it in danger from evil which attacks it from within its own household. . . . They will guard it and keep it safe by day and night [see Jdt 7:5], in life and in death."[23] The cleric is the city's ruler as well as watchman. "But," Bernard makes clear, "they made you a prince for their own sake, not yours."[24] Like a prince, the clergy must engage in battle to win over their people. They thus assume the role of "those spiritual men in the Church who make war with the sword of the Spirit, the word of God [see Eph 6:17], against their impious brothers."[25]

Whatever image Bernard employs in describing the clerical office and order, his message is the same: "Give heed, you who have been chosen for this ministry [see Eph 4:12; Ac 1:17]. Give heed, I say, to yourselves and the precious charge which has been entrusted to you. She [the Church] is a city; watch then and keep her in peace and safety. She is a bride; see to her adornment. She is a sheepfold; see that the sheep are pastured."[26]

B. CLERICAL MINISTRY

The Church must be served, be she seen through the image of city, bride, or sheepfold. Bernard insists that "the care of the city must be threefold to be effective. It must be protected from the violence of tyrants, from the snares of heretics, from the temptations of evil spirits."[27] Likewise "the bride must be adorned with the threefold adornments of good works, good character, and good disposition."[28] The service that must be given to the sheepfold Bernard explicates still more fully:

> ...The sheep must be pastured on the Scriptures which are the Lord's legacy. There are differences between the scriptural pastures. The commandments are the rough grasses intended for the stubborn and unspiritual as a guide to life and discipline [see Si 45:6]. There is the lush grass of dispensations granted out of mercy to the weak and timid. There is the strong, solid grass of counsel provided for the healthy who are able to distinguish between good and evil [see Heb 5:14]. The young, the lambs, must be given the milk of encouragement to drink, not solid food [see 1 Cor 3:2].[29]

The clergy, then, must provide the Church justice, the right order within which they can instruct their charges in virtue by preaching, counseling, and encouragement.

Through preaching, the cleric, as bride of Christ and mother of his spiritual children, feeds the needy with the milk of doctrine.[30] That doctrine is contained above all in the Scriptures, and in preaching the Gospel the cleric fulfills the role of shepherd.[31] The instruction in faith and holiness that the flock needs is provided by the Bridegroom's friends, who are also the city's watchmen:

> But, someone says: "How shall she believe without a preacher [see Rom 10:14], since faith comes by hearing [see Rom 10:17] and hearing comes by the word of a preacher?" God provides for this [see Gn 22:8]. Look, they are here already, they who are to instruct the new bride in the things she must know, prepare her for her marriage to the heavenly Bridegroom [see Rv 21:2], teach her the faith, and counsel her in the ways of holiness and true religion. Hear what the bride says: "The watchmen who guard the city have found me [Sg 3:3]."[32]

A sure model for the preacher is John the Baptist, who "shone forth ... by his example, by pointing the way, by his words—showing us himself by his actions, ourselves by his preaching."[33] Unlike John, who "was taught by inspiration," other folk must be "taught by preaching."[34] Like John, the preacher must be filled with salt's seasoning to accomplish his goal: the salvation, the happiness of all. For "a discourse seasoned with salt [see Col 4:6] is both pleasing to the taste and profitable to salvation."[35] Thus, Bernard's clergy are to preach the faith to their flocks and teach them the path to perfection. They are to reveal the nature of reality and show their folk how they are to respond to that reality.

But this is not all. Bernard's clergy labor to bring about Christian justice in the world—in *this* world. They must work to accomplish right order in the conditions and relationships in and within society:

> ... They present themselves as John to kings [see Mt 14:4], Moses to the Egyptians [see Ex 5:1ff.], Phineas to fornicators [see Nm 25:6–9], Elijah to idolaters [see 1 K 18:16–40], Elisha to the covetous [see 2 K 5:20–27], Peter to liars [see Ac 5:1–11], Paul to blasphemers [see Ac 13:45–46; 18:6], and as Christ to those who traffic in holy things [see Mt 21:12–13]. They do not despise the common folk but teach

them; they do not flatter the rich but overawe them; they do
not burden the poor but look after them; they do not fear the
threats of kings but scorn them . . . .[36]

Justice requires a judge, and Bernard assigns the role of spiritual
judge to the clergy. To them he turns when the right order of society
is threatened: "I hasten to you whose duty it is to judge all things in
this present time . . . ."[37]

Bernard presents a model for all clergy in the person of Malachy
of Armagh, whose legatine reformation of the Irish Church Bernard
finds profoundly instructive:

> . . . He does not relish honor; he does his duty as legate. Vari-
> ous assemblies are held in various places, so that no region,
> or part of a region, should be cheated of the fruit and benefit
> of his legation. . . . There is no one who can hide himself [see
> Ps 18:7] from his solicitous care. Neither sex, nor age, nor
> condition, nor profession makes any difference. . . . He cries
> out to the wicked: "Do not act wickedly," and to sinners:
> "Lift not up the horn [Ps 74:5]."[38]

Malachy labors mightily to reform individuals, the Church, and society: "Religion is planted everywhere; it takes root, and he nurses it
along. His eyes are on them [see Ps 32:18]; his care is for their
needs. In the councils, held far and wide, they revive the ancient
practices which, once held profitable, have been abolished through
the negligence of the priests. Not only are old practices brought
back, but new ones too are hammered out . . . ."[39]

Bernard would have other prelates imitate Malachy, charging
them with the function of holding together Christian communities in
structures that provide them justice:

> By "houses [see Sg 1:16]" understand the ordinary commu-
> nities of Christians. Those who hold high office [see 1 Tm
> 2:2] . . . strongly bind them together with laws justly imposed,
> as beams bind walls, lest, living by their own law and will,
> they should fall apart like tilting walls and tottering fences

[see Ps 61:4] and the whole building fall to the ground and be destroyed.[40]

Prelates are to support and sustain their clergy in their common effort to keep the houses of the Lord in good condition: "The panels firmly attached to the beams add impressively to the beauty of the house. And this seems to designate the courteous and disciplined behavior of a well-educated clergy who carry out their duties correctly. For how shall the clerical orders stand and fulfill their duties unless sustained, as by beams, by the beneficence and munificence of those whose power enables them to govern and protect?"[41]

Each bishop must oversee the good order of his house, of his Church, and of the clergy who serve it. The bishop of Rome must do the same, though he has a special charge: to oversee the right order of the whole Church.[42] In his care for the whole Church, the pope must take care to serve the cause of justice, not attack right order by assuming a lord's role over the other bishops: "Before everything else, you should consider that the holy Roman Church, in which God has established you as president, is the mother of churches, not the mistress. Consider that you are not the lord of the bishops but one of them, that you are the brother of those who love God and the companion of those who fear him."[43] Like the other bishops, the pope must see to it that his own household is in order, so "that those whom you have in your sight may be ordered and organized as a mirror and model of all honesty and order."[44]

With their own houses in right order, each bishop and his clergy can protect the liberty of the Church from those who would attack her freedom to promote justice.[45] The Church's freedom must be won, often from laymen; otherwise reform is impossible and justice will languish. And thus Bernard applauds an archbishop of Trier for his struggles to free a monastery from lay control and to reform its unwilling inhabitants.[46] In the cause of justice, for the freedom of the Church, the clergy must exhibit the fortitude of John the Baptist in rebuking even monarchs.[47]

Justice requires peace as well as freedom. Bernard sees the clergy as preeminent peacemakers. He tells them: "Yours is an apostolate of peace . . . ."[48] Again, Malachy of Armagh is the model. Malachy reconciles kings and their hostile nobles; he brings peace to warring peoples. He is also quite willing to employ the peace-making means of the society in which finds himself, restoring peace through the "granting and receiving of security and through oaths binding on both parties."[49] When nothing else will avail the cause of peace, Malachy is willing to gather an army to enforce peace and justice.[50]

The peace and justice that Bernard would have the clergy foster is internal as well as external. They must correct the evil actions of individuals as well as reform society and Church.[51] "Losses to the Lord's flock" must be the individual and collective concern of the clergy, who must "convene concerning the people's sins"; otherwise "a soul perishes and there is no one who gives it a thought."[52] Malachy of Armagh is once more the model Bernard presents: "Although his people were all wolves and no sheep, the shepherd stood in their midst undaunted, ingenious in every ruse by which to make wolves into sheep. This he accomplished by admonishing them in a body, by arguing privately, by weeping with each individual—sometimes roughly, sometimes gently, whichever way he saw was best for each one."[53] Concern for the sins of his flock does not drive Malachy to unremitting harshness. He adjusts his admonitions to his audience, and this is the reason "why priests, as ministers of the Word, must be solicitous to use toward erring hearts such moderation in words of reproach and fear as will not frighten them away from confessing. Let them open hearts in such a way that they do not stop mouths...."[54] Whether through admonishing or weeping or praying, the pastor's counsel should be characterized by "paternal consolation."[55]

The pastor must also be paternal in his care for the poor: "The father of the poor and the lover of poverty will not turn away from the prayers of the poor."[56] Far "from despoiling widow and orphan,"[57] the pastor should imitate Thurstan, the archbishop of York, whom God "inspired and girded...for the protection of the poor...."[58]

The clergy must minister to another sort of the needy, those whose needs stem from lack of the true faith. "Heresies have now arisen," Bernard points out to the clergy, and he counsels that they not "be found to have done less than the great bishops, your predecessors...."[59] The pastor must do battle against the heretic with "the weapon of holy preaching by which he shoots the warrior's sharpened arrows which are the efficacious words of the Holy Spirit."[60] That preaching must be public, "for an error publicly refuted does not spring up again, and falsehood revealed does not take root."[61] But, Bernard insists, those found in error should be taught, not fought with force:

> ...Heretics are to be caught rather than driven away. They are to be caught, I repeat, not by force of arms but by arguments by which their errors may be refuted. If possible, they themselves should be reconciled with Catholics and called back to the true faith. This is his [God's] will [see Jn 6:39–40]: "He wants all folk saved and brought to knowledge of the truth [1 Tm 2:4]."[62]

The cleric's intention should be God's: to serve heretics so that they may possess the truth that will make them free.

Bernard sees the office of the clergy as one of manifold ministry to all. He writes to his spiritual son Eugenius:

> You ought to be a model of justice, a mirror of holiness, an exemplar of piety. You should be a preacher of truth, a defender of the faith, the teacher of the nations [see 1 Tm 2:7]. You should be the leader of Christians, a friend of the Bridegroom [see Jn 3:29], an attendant of the bride. You should be the leader of the clergy and the shepherd of the people. You must be the instructor of the foolish [see Rom 2:20], the refuge of the oppressed, the advocate of the poor, the hope of the unfortunate, the protector of orphans, the judge of widows [see Ps 67:6; Lk 18:2–8], the eye of the blind [see Is 29:18], the tongue of the mute [see Is 35:6], the support of the aged [see Tb 5:23]. You must be the avenger of crimes, the terror of evil folk, the glory of the good, the staff of the powerful [see Ps 109:2], the hammer of tyrants, the father of kings. You ought to be the moderator of laws and the dispenser from canons. You should be the salt of the

earth [see Mt 5:13], the light of the world [see Jn 12:46], the priest of the Most High [see Gn 14:18], the vicar of Christ, the anointed of the Lord, and, finally, the god of Pharaoh [see Ex 7:1].[63]

Clerics who forget their ministry for their position and authority will face reproof,[64] but those who accept the noble burden of clerical office will find themselves rewarded by the master in whose vineyard they labor: "Happy the man who can say: 'I have labored more than all [1 Cor 15:10].' This is glory, but there is nothing vain in it, nothing weak, nothing boastful. If the labor is terrifying, let the reward be an enticement: 'For each shall be rewarded according to his labor [1 Cor 3:8].' Even if the apostle [Paul] has labored more than all, still he has not completed the entire task. There is still a place for you."[65]

IV
Noah's Many Virtues

He who is Christ's minister follows Christ [see Jn 12:26],"[1] and, of course, to follow him is to imitate not only his ministry but also his virtue. Bernard writes: "You will honor your ministry not by wearing fine garments, not by the splendor of your entourage, not by the size of your buildings. You will honor your ministry by honorable conduct, by concern for spiritual matters, and by the practice of good works."[2] Christian communities are like houses that require bishops with the strength of cedar beams and clergy with the virtues of cypress paneling:

> ...These timbers...possess natural properties which make them like the two orders [of prelates and clergy]. The cedar, an incorruptible and fragrant wood of great height, indicates well the qualities of the men to be selected as beams. Those appointed over others must be strong and reliable, tenacious in hope, with minds directed toward heavenly truths, radiating everywhere the good odor of their faith and conduct. With the apostle they can say that they are the incense everywhere offered to God by Christ [see 2 Cor 2:15]. The cypress, a wood equally incorruptible and fragrant, shows every cleric must be unblemished in his life and faith so he may be seen as a panel decorating the beauty of the house.[3]

Clergy overflowing with the virtues of Christ make the good and useful pastors whom Bernard acknowledges—at least rhetorically—

are rare birds.[4] However, he does not expect the clergy to be sinless but, rather, to be making an effort to progress toward virtue.[5] And Bernard is confident that God will provide assistance toward virtue even to those who have been placed in office without it.[6] Secure in the knowledge that God will provide him what he lacks, the cleric must strive for the virtue necessary to his office. Bernard counsels:

> Set your ways straight; strive to do good [see Jer 7:3] in your ministry. If holiness has not preceded [your election], at least it will follow. Then truly we shall acknowledge that you have been given the blessings of sweetness [see Ps 20:4], hoping for still better gifts for you. We shall be glad and rejoice [see Sg 1:3] because you will have been made a faithful and wise servant of the Lord's family [see Mt 24:45]. You will be a happy and powerful son whom the Father will place over all his goods [see Mt 24:47].[7]

The virtues bestowed on, and thus acquired by, the clergy are the means through which God cares for his people: "The pastors and teachers appointed for the people ought to be kind, powerful, and, especially, wise. Kind, so they may receive me pleasantly and mercifully. Powerful, so they may protect me securely. Wise, so they may lead me to and along the path which leads to the [heavenly] city [see Ac 12:10]."[8] With that kindness, power, and wisdom, the pastor must serve himself as well as others. Bernard writes Pope Eugenius:

> If you wish to belong totally to all, in the likeness of him who was made all things to all [see 1 Cor 9:22], I praise your devotion to humankind—but only if it is complete. You too are a human. For your devotion to be complete, let yourself be gathered to that breast which receives everyone. Otherwise, as the Lord says: "What does it profit you to gain the whole world but lose yourself alone [Mt 16:26]?" Since everyone possesses you, make sure you are one of those who possesses. Why should you alone be cheated of your service? ...You are indebted to the wise and the foolish [see Rom 1:14]; do you deny yourself alone?[9]

But to serve himself and others, the cleric must know himself; he must possess humility.

A. The Humble Cleric

In humility, the cleric knows both his dignity and weakness as a human being.[10] Humility is an especially difficult virtue for one whose clerical office places him in a position of preeminence. He must guard himself with special care against the self-deception, the pride which is humility's opposite.[11] Humble service, not the assertion and imposition of dominance, is the proper role of the cleric. So, Bernard warns: "You who have been placed on high, 'be not high-minded, but fear [Rom 11:20].' ... Know that your Church has been entrusted to you not as a handmaiden to a lord but ... as a mother to a son, as Mary to John . . . ."[12]

To attain the humility requisite to effective service, Bernard maintains, the wise cleric sets aside time to meditate, to ponder who and what he is.[13] He must look up to heaven to gain a proper perspective on his life and ministry:

> If the priest is a shepherd and the people are his flock, should the shepherd appear no different than his sheep? Will my shepherd go along like me, a poor sheep, walking with head to the ground, looking always at earth, empty-headed, thinking only of his stomach? . . . Woe to me when the wolf comes! No one will be there to run up, having foreseen the attack, and snatch me from his teeth. Should the shepherd live only by his senses, attached to the lowliest things, yearning only for the good of the earth? Should he not stand up like a man, look up to heaven, and seek and taste the things "which are above, not those on the earth [Col 3:1–2]"?[14]

To fight for his sheep, the shepherd must "gird himself again for the spiritual contest." He must "don the weapons so mighty with God [see Eph 6:10–11], . . . [among them] the leisure for meditation and application to prayer . . . ."[15] Malachy of Armagh again is the model:

"... The time he dedicated to leisure he spent without rest. How could he rest when he was employed in the Lord's justifications [see Ps 118:23]? Whenever he had time free from the needs of the people, he took no holiday from holy meditation or the pursuit of prayer or the leisure of contemplation."[16]

The objects of the cleric's meditation or consideration should be many. Bernard counsels: "To achieve the fruits of consideration, I think you should consider four things: yourself, what is below you, what is around you, and what is above you."[17] The cleric should begin his meditation with himself so he "does not reach out to other things in vain because he has neglected himself."[18] This meditation on oneself "has three divisions: You should consider what you are, who you are, and what sort of person you are. Consider what you are by nature, who you are in person, what sort of person you are in character."[19] The cleric must meditate on those things below him, the objects of his ministry,[20] and those things around him, the means he possesses to fulfill that ministry.[21] All this is put in proper perspective by meditation on those things above him: consideration of God, the Trinity, Christ, and the angels.[22]

Meditation on oneself is especially fruitful: "Bring a mirror and let a dirty face recognize itself. ... Even though there are things [in the reflection] of which you can be justly pleased, look at yourself closely and see if there is anything which ought to displease you. I wish you to glory in the testimony of your conscience [see 2 Cor 1:12], but I also wish you to be humbled by it."[23] The cleric will put his life and ministry in proper perspective if he meditates on the shortness of that life and ministry. Bernard urges him: "Join your meditations on the blandishments of this fleeting glory to the remembrance of 'your last end [Si 7:40].' Without doubt you will follow in death those whom you have succeeded in the [presidential] chair."[24] If the cleric will but bring to his meditations "an eye that is pure and simple [see Lk 11:34],"[25] he, like King David, will be able to make his ministry fruitful: "Whatever was appropriate in all matters he [David] was able to learn from the mystery of wisdom by an eager and inquiring mind; he imparted it for the salvation of men by zealous preaching ...."[26] The cleric's meditations bring him the humility that enables him to exercise a ministry of love.

B. The Cleric as Lover

The cleric who knows himself, both his glory and his weakness, will be able to see the glory and weakness of his flock in the light of love:

> A love like this is full of zeal. It is a love becoming to the Bridegroom's friend [see Jn 3:29], a love which must inspire the faithful and prudent servant whom the Lord appoints over his whole household [see Mt 24:45]. It fills the soul to capacity, grows hot, and overflows, gushing with abandon into streams. This is the love which cries out: "Who is weak and I am not weak? Who is scandalized and I am not inflamed [2 Cor 11:29]?" Let such a man preach, let him bear fruit; let him show new signs and do fresh wonders [see Si 36:6], for pride can find no hold in the man whom love possesses totally.... The man who has not attained this love is promoted to office at the gravest risk to himself, no matter how outstanding he is in other virtues.[27]

Filled with love, clerical Noahs may steer the ark in safety, for the ark is itself constructed of love.[28]

Love is the prerequisite virtue of those to whom, like Peter, the Lord entrusts his sheep:

> Not pointlessly did our Lord, in handing over the sheep, ask three times: "Peter, do you love me [Jn 21:17]?" It was, I think, as though Jesus had said: "Unless your conscience bears witness that you love [see Rom 9:1] me and love me so strongly and completely—more than you love your possessions, your family, even yourself—that my threefold command is fulfilled, you must not, on any account, take this charge upon you. Nor must you have any dealings with these, my sheep, for whom my blood was shed."[29]

Those chosen as shepherds must never lose their love of their flock through "despair at an end to the many demands made on ... [them], become callused and gradually lose their sense of ... compassion."[30]

Filled with compassionate love, the clergy will be able to mother their children with an inexhaustible flow of nourishment. For when their breasts "are drained dry, they are replenished from the maternal fount within and offered to all who would drink.... The number who drink from them, however great, cannot exhaust their content; their flow is never suspended, for they draw unceasingly from the inward fountain of love."[31]

But the love that bears fruit in the cleric's flock, in his children, must be coupled with reliance on the power of God, without whom the most compassionate love would be sterile.[32] The cleric should trust in God's goodness, knowing that God will supply what is lacking in his ministry and correct his mistakes.[33] Trust in God will keep the cleric from undue anxiety for his flock, and this in turn will free him for the leisure of meditation so necessary to fruitful ministry.[34]

C. THE GENEROUS SERVANT

If undue anxiety is not the minister's proper disposition, unstinting generosity in self-giving is:

> Be weak with the weak; be on fire with the scandalized [see 2 Cor 11:29]. If needed, become a Jew with the Jews [see 1 Cor 9:20].... Like Jeremiah [see Jer 43:6–7] and Ezekiel [see Ez 1:1–2], let yourself be taken captive into Egypt or the land of Chaldeans with the transgressors. Become with holy Job "the brother of the dragon and the companion of ostriches [Jb 30:29]." And, what is still more difficult, like Moses be blotted out of the Lord's book [see Ex 32:32]. Like Paul, have no fear "to be an anathema from Christ for the sake of the brethren [Rom 9:3]"....[35]

The cleric's generosity must be total, Bernard teaches, but must include himself as well as his flock: "We must be warned not to give away what we have received for our own welfare, or retain for ourselves what must be expended for others."[36] Thus, discretion is essential to proper self-giving.[37]

The Lord's good servant must not only give himself, he must give of his goods:

> Shall a bishop not be praised who freely parts with his goods and generously distributes them? This bishop does not wait for death when he would have no power to give or retain, as do many whose wills are not executed until they are dead [see Heb 9:17].... While still living he distributes freely and gives to the poor that his justice may remain for ever and ever [see Ps 111:9].... For the priests of God are "clothed with justice [Ps 131:9]" far more properly and richly than with gold or silk.[38]

The generous servant should not "burden the poor but look after them...."[39] Bernard advises a cleric who has become a burden to himself: "...Because you have set yourself up against God,...distribute to the poor [see Lk 18:22], and, because you have been merciful, you will obtain mercy [see Mt 5:7]."[40]

A life-long, humble commitment to the poor finds models throughout the history of the Church, from its beginnings to the present: "Who will grant me, before I die," Bernard exclaims, "to see the Church of God 'as in days of old [Is 51:9]' when the apostles let down their nets to catch [see Lk 5:4] not silver or gold but souls."[41] Martin of Tours followed this apostolic pattern and thus became himself a model by sharing his cloak with Christ in a beggar's disguise.[42] In Bernard's own day, too, Malachy of Armagh found his inspiration to generosity in the apostles. Bernard writes in his *Life of Malachy:* "Show me the man who is content with bare necessities, who despises superfluities! Yet this law was handed down from the apostles to their successors: 'Having food and clothing,' they said, 'let us be content with these [1 Tm 6:8].'"[43] And Malachy followed their apostolic pattern: "From the first day of his conversion to the end of his life he lived with nothing of his own. He had no man-servants nor maid-servants [see Gn 32:5]. He had no villages, hamlets, or any sort of revenue, whether ecclesiastical or secular, even when he was a bishop. Nothing was appropriated or assigned to him from which this bishop might live. He did not even have a house of his own."[44] Bernard is confident that in his day there are indeed clergy who follow the apostles, and saints Martin and Malachy, in giving of themselves and their goods: "I am sure you have not neglected to carry water to the thirsty and bread to meet fugitive folk [see Is 21:14]. I am sure you have not neglected the office of humanity, the cultivation of happiness, by which you refresh the vitals of Christ in his poor."[45]

D. THE CHASTE AND OBEDIENT MINISTER

To fulfill his ministry with whole-hearted generosity, Bernard's cleric must be chaste: "Would that those who are incapable of remaining chaste would fear to profess perfection rashly and assume the name of celibate. This is a costly tower, a great precept, which not everyone can accept [see Mt 19:11]. Without doubt it is better to marry than burn [see 1 Cor 7:9], to be saved among the ranks of the faithful than to live less worthily in lofty clerical ranks and be more severely judged."[46] Priestly chastity is an "adornment... making the priest beloved of God and [his] folk [see Si 45:1]...."[47] But chastity must be an expression of love; for "without love chastity has no value or merit.... Chastity without love is a lamp without oil. Take away the oil and the lamp does not shine. Take away love and chastity is not pleasing."[48]

And the chastity most important to the priest is purity of heart, which is single-minded love for God and neighbor,[49] for "he who possesses a pure heart and a good conscience may securely abandon himself, even lose himself, to win others."[50] With purity of heart, the priest will preach in a manner pleasing to God: "Do you ask whom I call impure? Anyone who looks for human praise, who does not deliver the Gospel without charge [see 1 Cor 9:18], who preaches for profit, who considers godliness a means of gain [see 1 Tm 6:5], who does not work for fruit but gifts."[51]

Thus the ministry of the pure of heart must be the expression of well-regulated love. And that ordering is accomplished through the virtue of obedience, so that "whenever necessity arises and they [the clergy] are commanded to be ambassadors for Christ [see 2 Cor

5:20], they do not refuse."[52] Those whose ministry confers authority must respect the authority of others.[53] Bernard writes:

> I cannot wonder enough at the careful and humble faith and response which [the centurion] made to our Savior: "For I am a man subject to authority, having soldiers subject to me [Mt 8:9]." O man of prudent and truly humble heart! Before explaining that he is in charge of soldiers, he suppresses any self-exaltation by his profession that he himself is subject to authority. Indeed, he puts forth first his subjection because it is more important than his authority.[54]

E. THE INDUSTRIOUS LABORER

The worker in the Lord's vineyard must apply himself with vigor to his labor. Bernard admonishes clerics, in this case the pope: "You must flee idleness, the mother of frivolity and the stepmother of the virtues."[55] The faithful cleric must be industrious in his ministry: "My dear friend, you must act in a manner befitting the office you hold and the dignity you have accepted. Labor manfully and prudently, according to the Lord's zeal in you, for his glory, your salvation, and the benefit of many in the holy Church. Then you can say that 'the grace of God in me has not been fruitless [1 Cor 15:10].'"[56] The industrious cleric must also work hard as a warrior "who has two battles to fight, one for himself and the other for those entrusted to him."[57] In fighting the good fight, the cleric must realize that he cannot do everything. He must acknowledge that his worthy goals are often unattainable and thus necessarily unattained.[58] Industry, not anxiety, should motivate the laborer's work.

F. THE JUST AND PRUDENT LEADER

To fulfill his ministry, the cleric must possess "holiness of life and zeal for justice...."[59] Bernard urges the cleric to meditation on justice, a meditation that "guides the mind into conformity with this virtue. The mind must reflect in order to deduce the norm of justice, which is not to do to another what one would not wish done to oneself or deny another what one wishes for oneself [see Mt 7:12]. In these two rules the entire nature of justice is made clear."[60] This definition allows a conflation of justice and mercy. For both the cleric must be zealous. In a letter to Pope Eugenius he writes:

> Your apostolate is capable of zeal for both justice and mercy. The honor of majesty loves justice, but God forbid that it prejudices mercy. The steward [see Lk 16:1–9] "who is praised in the Gospel [2 Cor 8:18]" preferred to defraud his lord rather than deny his neighbor mercy. For a hundred he accepted eighty on one occasion, and fifty on another. He was justly praised for preferring the loss of his lord's goods to the loss of his neighbor. A person who does this deserves his reward; by one act he made friends of those whom he kept as servants.[61]

True justice thus includes mercy, and the proper application of justice requires prudence: "You have been made a watchman on the housetops of Israel [Ez 3:17]; your work is prudence."[62] Prudence is a virtue requiring maturity; no one without this maturity should be given extensive authority over others. Bernard quotes his former monk, Pope Eugenius III: "We forbid that...[clerical] honors be conferred on young men or those in lesser orders, but rather on those distinguished by their prudence and their worthy lives."[63] Prudence, like justice, is a virtue born in meditation.[64] It enables the cleric to correct evils wisely, moderately: "You cannot correct every error at once or suddenly reduce excess to moderation. You will have the opportunity at the right time to pursue this little by little, according to the wisdom given you by God [see 2 Pt 3:15]. In the meantime, do what you can to use others' evils for good."[65]

Prudence will confer its own fruits on the cleric. Through prudence he will learn to be patient and peaceable. Bernard writes to Hugh, the archbishop of Rouen:

Now that you live among the people of Rouen your task is patience.... You must have patience so you will not be overcome by evil; you must also be peaceable to overcome evil with good [see Rom 12:21]. In patience you will bear those who are evil; by being peaceable you will heal those whom you bear. In patience you will possess your soul [see Lk 21:19]; by being peaceable you will possess the souls of those entrusted to you.... So be patient when you are with those who are evil; be peaceable, for you must preside over the evil. Love should be zealous, but for now moderate your severity. Do not avoid correction, but postponement is more profitable. The vigor of justice is always fiery but never hasty.[66]

Bernard's model of the peaceable cleric is Martin of Tours. Bernard quotes Martin's biographer, Sulpitius: "He exercised such patience with all injuries that, although he was bishop, even the least of his clerics could offend him with impunity. He did not remove them from office. As far as depended on him, he did not exclude them from his love...."[67] The cleric who would serve his flock well must, then, be both peaceable and patient. To guide his flock peaceably and patiently, he must be prudent. And prudence is the virtue that brings to fruition his justice and mercy.

G. THE COMPLETE CLERIC

The cleric who possesses these virtues, or who is striving to attain them, should be confident in his calling. And, Bernard asks: "What is this calling but an inward impulse of love inciting us to zeal for our brethren's salvation, to zeal for the beauty of God's house [see Ps 25:8], to zeal for an increase in the fruits of his righteousness [see 2 Cor 9:10], to zeal in the praise and glory of his name [see Phil 1:11]?"[68] Moved by these motives, the cleric "may believe with certainty... that the Bridegroom is present, inviting him again and again to the vineyards."[69] This invitation, this calling, this vocation brought a life-long response from Malachy of Armagh:

... Blind and improvident, death has tied Malachy's tongue, shackled his footsteps, relaxed his hands, and closed his eyes. Those faithful eyes, I say, which by their tender, loving tears had brought divine grace to sinners. Those undefiled hands which had loved always to be used in laborious and humble deeds,... which had been lifted up to heaven in prayer without anger or contention [see 1 Tm 2:8], which had conferred many blessings on the sick.... The beautiful footsteps of him who preached the gospel of peace and brought glad tidings of good things [see Rom 10:15; Is 52:7]. The feet often wearied in zeal for loving mercy.... And lastly, those priest's holy lips which guarded knowledge [see Mal 2:7], the mouth of the just which meditated wisdom, the tongue which spoke judgment [see Ps 36:30], yes, and mercy too [see Ps 100:1]. By these he would cure great wounds in souls.[70]

Clerics who remain constant in their pastoral calling—as did Malachy—will receive their reward from the Shepherd of all sheepfolds.[71]

The sort of cleric who will receive that reward Bernard describes in a glowing passage from his *On Consideration:*

... They are not impudent, but modest and respectful. Besides God alone they fear nothing; they hope for nothing except from God. They do not look to the hands of those who approach, but to their needs. They stand up manfully for the afflicted and judge fairly for the meek of the earth [see Is 11:4]. They are composed in character, proven in holiness, ready for obedience, gentle in patience. They are submissive to discipline, stern in censuring, catholic in faith, faithful in service. They are of one mind toward peace and alike in unity. They are upright in judgment, farsighted in counsel, prudent in commands, industrious in organization, energetic in action, modest in speech. They are fearless in adversity, faithful in prosperity, sober in zeal, not remiss in mercy. They are not idle in their leisure, not frivolous in their hospitality, not extravagant in their entertainment. They are not anxious in the care of their own property, not eager for that of another or wasteful with their own. Everywhere and in all things they are considerate . . . .[72]

Such men Bernard is happy to have as the Noahs who guide the ark of the Church.[73]

V

The Lay Order of Job

A. THE BLESSINGS OF MARRIED LIFE

*T*hose to whom the Noahs minister are the Jobs, the lay folk, the people of God. Bernard often refers to them as married folk, an accurate description for most of them: "Then there are the married folk, who do not transgress the commandments, so that they may be called justly the people of God [see Ps 84:9] and the sheep of his pasture [see Ps 94:7]."¹ Although "virginity is a praiseworthy virtue,"² Bernard knows that "those who are content to contract a legitimate marriage do not think they have abandoned the Gospel in not choosing to follow the sublime counsel of celibacy...."³

The faithful are free to choose the married life, for it is not merely lawful, it is a source of abundant blessing. Addressing those heretics who insist that marriage be reserved to virgins, Bernard writes: "Why do you limit the abundant blessings of marriage? Why do you restrict to the virgin the right granted to all her sex? Paul would not permit it unless it were lawful. But 'permit' is an understatement; he also commends it. 'I wish,' he says, 'the younger women to marry [1 Tm 5:14],' and there is no doubt that he includes widows."⁴ The free choice of marriage makes of it a lifestyle wholly good: "Marriage is neither enjoined nor forbidden, but once contracted it cannot be dissolved. What, therefore, before the nuptials was clearly an open option, becomes for the married wholly good."⁵ The bond thus established is a strong one. Bernard writes: "I think that the bond which links an abbot with his disciples is not stronger nor more binding than the bond which God has tied between married folk with an inviolable sacrament. As the Savior says: 'What God has joined together, humans may not separate [Mt 19:6].'"[6] True marriage is a freely chosen sacrament.

Love is the tie that unites woman and man in the dignity of married life, a dignity which Bernard convincingly affirms in the preface to one of his letters. He writes: "Bernard, abbot of Clairvaux, to his beloved Marius and his wife. May you love one another and thus nourish one another by placing first the love of Christ."[7] Love for one another is the efficacious means by which married folk come to their loving Savior.

Married love is not simply a matter of the will, though it is surely that. The love between a woman and a man requires more than a desire for the well-being of the other; it demands an affection which is nourished and properly expressed by physical intimacy. The embraces of married couples are the chaste expressions of a mutual love that strengthens them in their love for Christ. Bernard writes to Simon and Adelaide, the duke and duchess of Lotharingia: ". . . May you delight in one another in chaste and loving embrace, so that the sole love of Christ holds sway in each of you."[8]

There is no sin, or even fault, in the intimacies of husband and wife: ". . . If spouse embrace spouse, there is surely no fault in it."[9] Bernard writes of the heretical teaching that sexual intimacy in marriage is shameful: "Take away from the Church honorable marriage and [you also do away with] the stainless marriage bed [see Heb 13:4] . . . ."[10] For Bernard, sexual intimacy is a proper component of marriage,[11] and has been so since the beginning of humankind: "Physical unity is between man and woman, of whom it is said [in Gn 2:24] 'They shall be two in one flesh.'"[12]

Love, Bernard believes, is the proper way the will should choose,[13] and this choice presupposes that the intellect knows the object of the choice.[14] But married love encompasses more; it also involves the feelings in an intimate relationship which Bernard calls friendship.[15] And married love is properly expressed in physical intimacy. Marriage thus involves the whole person, soul and body, in a loving relationship.

Much of Bernard's teaching about ideal married love can be derived from his description of the relationship of the Bridegroom and bride in his *Sermons on the Song of Songs*. As Jean Leclercq has written: "St. Bernard draws a close parallel between 'fleshly union' *(carnale connubium)* and 'spiritual marriage' *(spirituale matrimonium)*. The analogy is based on a constant and realistic description of conjugal love."[16] Bernard himself writes:

> The soul...now ventures to think of marriage. Why should she not, when she sees that she is like him [the Bridegroom] and therefore ready for marriage?...Her declaration of love is a betrothal....The apostles followed this when they said: "See, we have left everything to follow you [Mt 19:27]." There is a similar saying which, pointing to the spiritual marriage between Christ and the Church, refers to physical marriage: "For this shall a man leave his father and mother and be joined to his wife, and the two shall be one flesh [Eph 5:31; see Gn 2:24]."...When you see a soul leaving everything [see Lk 5:11] and clinging to the Word with all her heart and desire, living for the Word,...ruling her life by the Word, conceiving by the Word,...you know that the soul is the spouse and bride of the Word. The heart of the Bridegroom has faith [see Prv 31:11] in her, knowing her to be faithful, for she has rejected all things as dross to gain him [see Phil 3:8].[17]

It is faithful love that makes a marriage.

Even unfaithfulness will be overcome by the tender forgiveness that loving spouses show for one another. Of this Bernard writes:

> Since I love, I cannot doubt that I am loved, any more than I can doubt that I love. Nor can I fear to look on his face, since I have sensed his tenderness. In what have I known it? In this: not only has he sought me as I am, but he has shown me tenderness and caused me to seek him with confidence. How can I not respond to the search, to which I respond with tenderness? How can he be angry with me when he has overlooked the contempt I showed for him?[18]

The love of the spouses overcomes all and leads to a friendship that conforms the spouses to each other in everything:

> When she loves perfectly, the soul is wedded to the Word.
> ...What is more desirable than love, by the operation of which, O soul,...you approach the Word with confidence, cling to him with constancy, speak to him as a familiar friend, and refer to him in every matter with an intellectual grasp proportionate to the boldness of your desire. Truly this is a spiritual contract, a holy marriage. It is more than a contract; it is an embrace, an embrace in which identity of will makes of two one spirit [see 1 Cor 6:17].[19]

Marital love is a transcending unity of wills in love, of intellects in regard for one another, of affections in friendship, and of bodies in embrace.

In true marriage there is an affinity between the spouses that informs their entire lives.[20] Between the spouses "all things are held in common; nothing belongs personally to either one or the other; there is no division. They share the same inheritance, the same table, the same home, the same marriage bed, even the same flesh."[21] For most, this sharing of bed and flesh will lead to the conception and birth of children. Bernard condemns contemporary heretics who teach that the products of sexual congress are unclean: "...What is the reason for this wholesale avoidance of everything produced by copulation?...I am inclined to say it is you [heretics] who are unclean when you brand anything as unclean in itself. 'To the pure, all things are pure,' says one clear thinker [Paul, in Ti 1:15]. Nothing is unclean except to one who thinks it unclean...."[22] Copulation and child-bearing are a means to salvation for married folk: "A woman shall be 'saved through child-bearing if she continues in faith [1 Tm 2:15].' Children shall be strengthened by the new birth of baptism [see Ti 3:5]. And adults not able to preserve continence shall be redeemed by the thirtyfold fruit of marriage [see Mt 13:8]."[23]

The love of the spouses overflows not only in conception and child-bearing, but also in the child-rearing which follows. It, too, is characterized by love, a love that overcomes all the difficulties of bringing up children to God. Bernard writes to the countess of Blois:

> I grieve that your son has behaved badly toward you. I deplore the conduct of the son as much as the wrong to his mother.... You must trust that the merits and alms-giving of his father will bring about a change for the better in him. You must besiege God more and more with prayers and promises on his behalf. For, even if he shows less filial devotion to you than he should, a mother ought not desert or lose her maternal affection for her offspring. "Can a mother forget the children of her womb [Is 49:15]?" ... Let us pray and "offer tears before the Lord [Ps 94:6]" that God will make such a naturally talented youth an imitator of the goodness of his parents. And this I do not doubt.[24]

Even the burden of adolescent children can be overcome by spouses who love.

Spouses can also be burdens to one another: "I am reminded now of the gospel scene in which our Lord instructs the apostles on the obligations of matrimony. At this, they exclaim: 'If this is the case, it is not wise to marry [Mt 19:10]!' Indeed, it is a difficult matter. If you hold on to what you have begun, nothing could be more burdensome; if you reject the invitation to do so, nothing could be less Christian."[25] Again, love will overcome all difficulties:

> Pure love has no self-interest. Pure love does not gain strength through expectation; it is not weakened by distrust. This is the love of the bride, for this is the bride—with all that means. Love is the being and hope of the bride. She is full of it, and the bridegroom is content with it.... So to love is marriage, for it is not possible so to love and be loved too little [in return]. Vigorous and perfect marriage consists in the harmony of the two.[26]

The dignity of marriage is shown by the "metaphorical transpositions"[27] that this loving relationship undergoes at the hands of

Bernard and other monastic authors. As Jean Leclercq has written,
Bernard

> maneuvers the transposition from one register to another by
> situating it on three different planes. First, love between the
> three Divine Persons, then between the Word and the
> Humanity of Christ, and finally the love exchanged between
> God, Christ, his Church, and each single member of the
> Church.... [Bernard and the other] monastic authors must
> have considered marriage as being great and beautiful since
> they saw it as the symbol of the most sublime mysteries.[28]

Married love is, in one sense, the most complete form of human
love, since it engages all the faculties of the soul—intellect, will, and
feelings—and the body as well.

B. MERCHANTS, MANUFACTURERS, AND THE PROFIT MOTIVE

Clerics are not the only folk who minister to the needs of Bernard's
Europe. The merchants and manufacturers who dwell in its cities and
towns minister to their fellows by making and trading those goods
which they need and want. And, despite his rural and aristocratic
background, Bernard has no quarrel with this "middle" class or its
activities. He addresses them with respect; to the people of Milan he
writes: "... Listen to me, you illustrious folk, you noble race, you
glorious city."[29] For Bernard, the profits that motivate the business
activities of the middle class are not squalid or sordid. In an effort to
enlist the middle class of Germany in the crusading effort, Bernard
appeals to the profit motive without denigrating it in the slightest:

> If you are a prudent merchant, if you are a "searcher of this
> world [1 Cor 1:20]," let me point out the great market pos-
> sibilities [of this venture] to you. See that you do not let
> them slip by you. Take the sign of the cross, and you will
> obtain remission for all the offenses which you confess with a
> contrite heart. If you buy the material [for the cross], it will

cost little. If you devotedly take it on your shoulder, it will
have the value of God's kingdom. So they do well who
receive this small, celestial sign. They do well, and it will
surely not be seen as folly in them [see Ps 21:3] if they hasten and seize for themselves that which will profit their salvation [see Ps 117:14].[30]

The profit motive is not evil; it can be morally good when directed
toward the ultimate reward.[31]

Bernard often expresses allegorically his positive evaluation of
middle-class activities—notably, in his use of the image of trading.
Bernard begins his seventh *Parable:* "The kingdom of heaven is like
a monk-businessman. When he hears a market will shortly be held,
he gathers his wares for display in the marketplace. He takes his
eight bundles [images of the eight beatitudes], loaded on his pack
animals...."[32] In the same *Parable,* Bernard identifies the monk-
businessman's teachers in trade: "His teacher is Luke, the Syrian
physician, who, as a doctor, knows what will profit him. But he does
not reveal to him the delights and riches which Matthew, my tax-
collector, prescribed while sitting in his tax office, for he was dedicated to making a profit in such matters, and he is a master teacher in
business such as this."[33]

Bernard recognizes the danger the middle class faces in its quest
for profit. He writes Innocent II that people of Cremona have been
hardened in their opposition to peace, and that "their prosperity is
their undoing...."[34] But, in themselves, riches are morally neutral;
their moral value lies in the use made of them. Bernard writes
another pope—this time Eugenius III:

What did the holy apostle [Peter] leave you?...I am sure of
one thing: it is neither gold nor silver, for he himself says: "I
do not have silver or gold [Ac 3:6]." If you happen to have
these, use them not for your own pleasure, but to meet the
needs of the time. In this way you will be using them as if
you were not using them [see 1 Cor 7:31]. When you consider the good of the soul, these things are neither good nor
bad. The [proper] use of them is good; the abuse is bad;

solicitude for them is worse; deriving [unjust] advantage from them is still more shameful.[35]

Motivation is thus the moral key to the acquisition and use of wealth.

Those who inordinately desire wealth, as if it were the end of human existence, "fall into the devil's net [see Ps 90:3]...."[36] That net is the unhappiness that results from the passionate pursuit of what will not satisfy one's deepest desire:

An insatiable love of riches, far from refreshing the soul by its exercise, racks it with desire. Acquisition is fraught with toil, possession with fear, loss with sorrow.... The proper use of wealth is when it goes to others; only the name and care are granted the rich. And for so little—or, rather, nothing at all—they despise the glory which eyes have not seen, ears have not heard, the human heart not conceived—the glory which God has prepared for those who love him [see 1 Cor 2:9].[37]

Those who seek riches as an end are a "generation which has not regulated its heart [see Ps 77:8]."[38] Bernard warns these "wretched slaves of Mammon [see Mt 6:24]: You cannot glory in the cross of our Lord Jesus Christ [see Gal 6:14] and at the same time trust in hoards of money; you cannot chase after gold [see 1 Tm 6:17] and taste how sweet is the Lord [see Ps 33:9]."[39] Those for whom money is the ultimate good are "the wicked who walk round in circles [see Ps 11:9], naturally wanting what will satisfy their desires, yet foolishly rejecting what will bring them to their true end, which lies not in consumption but in consummation."[40]

It is the inordinate desire for wealth, not the wealth itself, which is evil; so that the "rich of this world [see 1 Tm 6:17] must not imagine that, because Christ said: 'Blessed are the poor in spirit, for theirs is the kingdom of heaven [Mt 5:3],' Christ's brothers and sisters possess only heavenly gifts."[41] Riches, in the end, are irrelevant in the pursuit of happiness, for "to the faithful, the whole world is full of riches—the whole world because, whether in adversity or prosperity, all things serve them and cooperate for their good."[42] Members of all classes, and surely of the middle class, seek happiness as their end, but wealth properly sought is not a hindrance to that end.

Wealth must be not only properly sought but also properly used. Bernard writes Thurstan, the archbishop of York: "All the Church of the saints has told of your works of mercy and alms-giving. But this you have in common with many others, for this is the duty of all who possess the goods of this world."[43] The need of others presents an opportunity to all those blessed with wealth, as Bernard writes to Marius and his wife:

> Whatever you possess on earth, it is certain that, sooner or later, you will lose it all unless you take care to send it on to heaven by the hands of the poor. Through them, dearest friends, "store up treasures for yourselves in heaven, where moths cannot destroy them, where thieves cannot break in and steal [Mt 6:20]." . . . If you are concerned about couriers, you have not one but many who stand daily at your door. They will faithfully convey whatever you wish to send through them. God has multiplied their sorrows [see Gn 3:16] at this time, so that you have the opportunity of storing up treasure in a place of total happiness and security.[44]

But generosity toward the needy is not the only virtue Bernard urges on the manufacturers and merchants of his time. They, as city folk, should be devoted to peace but ready to defend their territory. Bernard writes the people of Milan: "I consider it no small honor for you that, through my intervention, you have turned toward peace and harmony with your neighbors, when, as the whole world knows, the hostile invasions of many cities have been powerless to force this on you."[45] In the pursuit of peace and justice, city-states—in this case Genoa—should persevere:

> And now nothing remains, dear friends, but to encourage you in perseverance, for by what other means do people merit glory, the crown of virtues? Clearly, without persever-ance victory cannot be won in battle and the rewards of vic-tory follow. . . . Take away perseverance and obedience will

have no reward, kindness no favor, valor no praise. It is not
the one who begins but "the one who will persevere to the
end who will be saved [Mt 24:13]." ... If Samson had perse-
vered in caution, Solomon in devotion, the former would
not have lost his strength, the latter his wisdom [see Jgs 16;
1 K 11].[46]

Love of peace, patience, obedience, kindness, humility, prudence, strength, devotion, and wisdom are thus the virtues of the
middle class—a demanding standard indeed! To these Bernard adds
respect for the authority of the princes who defend city-states.[47] In
short, the middle class must be as virtuous as monks, clergy, and
rulers[48] in order to fulfill their ministry of service to the people of
God.

C. The Nobility of Farmers and Craftsmen

There is still another ministry that Bernard recognizes—the most
basic ministry of all: the provision of food and other necessities for all
God's folk. But Bernard scarcely mentions farmers and craftsmen,
and this is probably due to the fact that their role is so necessary as to
be obvious. In one of his *Sentences,* Bernard says simply: "The feet,
which carry the entire body [of society], are the farmers; on their
labor live all the others...."[49] There are a few other, scattered references in Bernard's writings to the ministry of farmers and artisans—
always indirect, in the context of spiritual admonitions to monks and
to folk in general.

One such passage, from Bernard's moving lament at the death of
his brother—and brother monk—Gerard, shows Bernard's respect
for the dignity of agriculture and the trades of craftsmen:

Both in the greatest things and in the least he [Gerard] was
the greatest. For example, in the buildings, in the fields, in
the vegetable gardens, in the water systems—indeed, in all
the various arts and trades of country folk—who, I say, could
fail to see his skill in all this sort of work? He could easily

function as master to the masons, the carpenters and smiths, the farm workers, the gardeners, the shoemakers, and the weavers.[50]

All these functions are noble in Bernard's eyes. It comes as no surprise to him that Jesus himself was born into the family of a carpenter.[51]

Farmers and craftsmen, manufacturers and merchants, clerics and monks, all share the same goal, all are called to union with God. All those who seek God are the Church; all can become brides of Christ. All have their ministry, their tasks, in the vineyard of the Lord. Noah, Daniel, and Job—monks, clerics, and lay folk—are all called to a life of virtue and can cross the sea of life in safety and with the expectation of salvation. This is true, too, of those charged with the governance of society, those other members of the order of Job, the nobility.

VI

Job's Ministry of Governance

The governance of twelfth-century society was provided by a complex array of institutions, public, semi-public, and private. Though the complexity of this institutional arrangement may seem haphazard and bewildering to the modern observer, what is clear is that twelfth-century political institutions were largely served by the members of one social class, the class from which Bernard himself came.[1] Bernard himself made little analysis—and, for that matter, no criticism[2]—of contemporary political institutions, but he did comment extensively on the duties of the class charged with governance in his time—and on the virtues necessary to that class in the exercise of its function.

A. VASSALS OF THE LORD AND MINISTERS OF GOD

The house of God that is the Church requires governance, Bernard claims, "for, where a multitude are gathered together without any contract of peace, without the observance of law, without discipline and a ruling head, it is called not a people but a mob, not a state but confusion. It shows itself a Babylon; of Jerusalem it has nothing."[3] For Bernard, the state is as much a religious institution as is the institutional Church. Those charged with the governance of the state must consequently have as their chief goal the salvation of those who inhabit the land they rule. Bernard writes to Emperor Lothar:

Blessed be God, who chose you and has raised you up to be a horn of salvation for us [see Lk 1:69], for the praise and glory of his name and for the restoration of the glory of the Empire, for the support of the Church in an evil hour [see 2 M 1:5], and, finally, for the work of salvation in the midst of the earth [see Ps 73:12]. It is God's doing that the crown of your glory [see Is 28:5] is daily augmented and elevated, wonderfully growing and progressing in beauty and splendor before God and humankind [see Lk 2:52].[4]

Because the happiness of humankind is the common goal of the state and the Church, they are—or should be—mutually supportive institutions. Writing to Lothar's successor, Conrad, Bernard finds the model for this in the person of Jesus himself:

Kingship and priesthood could not be more sweetly, more agreeably, or more closely joined and united than in the person of the Lord, both coming together as equals—for he came to us in the flesh with both powers. Not only this, but he has so mingled and combined these powers in his body, which is the Christian people with himself as their head [see Col 1:18], that the apostle calls this people "a chosen race, a royal priesthood [1 Pt 2:9]."[5]

Bernard aims at translating this Christology into the world of political reality: "May I have no part in the counsels of those who say either that the peace and liberty of the churches will suffer from the Empire or that the prosperity and glory of the Empire will suffer from the churches. For God, the founder of both, did not join them for their mutual destruction but for their mutual support."[6] Thus the proper concern of the temporal ruler is "both to protect his crown and defend the Church"[7] in its ministry. For Bernard, this is what is meant by the passage in Matthew (22:21) that one should give to Caesar what is Caesar's and to God what is God's.[8]

And, if Caesar is to respect what is God's and defend the Church, this is only fitting, for God is the source of the ruler's power.[9] Because the source of the ruler's power is God, that power is not lightly opposed. But the people's obligation to respect that power is matched by the ruler's obligation to respect the source of his or her power.[10] Thus, as Bernard writes to Henry I, king of England, the ruler must "zealously serve" God, who is his and his people's "feudal lord."[11]

Rulers exercise their function as vassals of the Lord by serving their people as "the faithful ministers of God."[12] Only when they remain faithful to their Lord will their governing ministry be successful. Bernard writes to King Louis VI of France: "The kingdoms of the world and the rights of kingdoms will remain sound and unimpaired only if they do not contravene the divine ordinances and dispositions."[13] The ruler's devoted vassalage and faithful ministry ensure not only a sound kingdom but a heavenly reward: "May you continue so to administer your kingdom of France that afterwards you may acquire the kingdom of heaven . . . ."[14]

B. THE JUST RULER

Writing to Count Henry of Champagne, Bernard provides a list of those activities that will win the ruler a successful reign and a heavenly reward:

> For this "the Prince of the kings of the earth [Rv 1:5]" has set you up as a prince on earth, that under him and for him you may encourage the good, restrain the evil, defend the poor, and give "justice to those suffer wrongs [Ps 145:7]." If you do this, you will be doing the work of the Prince and have every reason to hope that God will increase and strengthen your principality. If you do not, you must fear that the very honor and power which you seem to have will be taken away from you—which God forbid![15]

Rulers, then, must provide their people the right order that is justice. And this means that rulers must provide legal recourse through their courts and preside with justice in them. Writing to Henry's father, Count Theobald of Champagne, Bernard affirms that his confidence in Theobald's sense of justice and law is so great "that

I think that not even your enemies would have cause to fear to plead their case in your court...."[16] In the cause of justice, the ruler must be willing to suffer. Writing to Pope Innocent II on Theobald's behalf, Bernard illustrates the plight of that prince:

> That great lover of innocence and practitioner of piety, Count Theobald, is almost at the mercy of his enemies [see Ps 40:3]. He has been struck that he might fall, but the Lord has supported him [see Ps 117:13]. And he rejoices that he serves the cause of justice in obedience to you, resting in the apostle who says: "If you suffer anything for the sake of justice, you are blessed [1 Pt 3:14]," and in the Gospel which says: "Blessed are they who suffer for justice's sake [Mt 5:10]."[17]

The price of justice may be high, but the ruler must be willing to pay that price.

Committed to the standard of justice, the ruler may expect God's assistance in attaining the goal of a well-ordered state.[18] Bernard counsels Louis VII of France that "it is better and safer that we leave all these things to the judgment and disposition of God, who can see to it that the good that he wishes will be done and stay done. And he can see to it that the evil which evil persons seek does not come about, or, rather, comes to those who desire and seek to do it."[19] Both extreme effort and trusting reliance on God are necessary to the rule of a just state and society.

Understandably, Bernard's quest for the proper administration of a society seeking justice sometimes finds its expression in complaints to the powerful against their unjust rule.[20] Peace and justice are the responsibility of the ruler; those who refuse to provide them are truly called tyrants. And Bernard does not hesitate to apply the term, at least three times, to Roger of Sicily.[21] Rulers who would reject tyranny must take special care to provide justice to the disadvantaged in the society to which they minister. Bernard admonishes Queen Melisande of Jerusalem: "Take care of pilgrims, the needy, and, especially, prisoners, 'for by such sacrifices God's favor is obtained [Heb 13:16].'"[22] For Melisande and others with her ministry of governance, the model in this is Jesus himself: "Learn from him, as a widow, that you might be gentle and humble in heart [see Mt 11:29]; learn from him, as a queen, for he 'judges the poor with justice and reproves with equity on behalf of the meek of the earth [Is 11:4].'"[23] And, in their care for the poor, rulers should seek to refer all to the same Lord.[24] Bernard would have the ruler exercise a definite preference for the poor: "... Love them, care for them, protect them, support them; for then you will stand securely before the tribunal of Christ [see Rom 14:10] if you have the poor to love you and intercede for you."[25]

Justice, which the ruler is to mete out to poor and rich alike, must be tempered by mercy. Bernard pleads with Count Theobald: "When I was passing through Bar the other day, I met a woman in a miserable condition—for her soul was in anguish [see 2 K 4:27]—and my heart was moved by her sorrows. She implored me with prayers and tears to intercede with you for her. She is the wife of that man of yours, Belinus, whom you have recently punished severely. Be merciful to her, that you may receive mercy from God [see Mt 5:7]."[26] And, perhaps testing Theobald's patience, Bernard adds still another request for mercy:

"Since I have begun, I will speak about this [too] to my lord [Gn 18:27]." Recently a duel was fought before the provost of Bar, and the vanquished had his eyes put out on the spot by your order. And, as if to be defeated and to have lost his eyes were a mere nothing, your ministers, so he complains, have taken away from him all his possessions. It is only just, if it pleases you, that his goods be restored to him by your mercy, so that his miserable life may be supported in some way. The sin of the father should not be imputed to his innocent children [see Ez 18:20], so that at least they may inherit the family home, if any.[27]

Mercy, then, is the opposite side of the coin of justice.[28] Mercy is so important to Bernard's view of justice that he sometimes counsels risking its bestowal on the unworthy.[29]

Protecting, supporting, and ensuring the worthiness of the Church are crucial tasks in the ruler's effort to ensure a just society. The ruler must be a "shield" against those who would attack the Church.[30] Councils and the churchmen assembled in them must be protected in their efforts to promote reform of the Church.[31] For Bernard, the good of the Church—her reform—is primarily served by ensuring the freedom of episcopal elections. And this is one of the tasks of the ruler. Bernard writes to King Stephen of England: "You must allow all elections to be conducted freely."[32] Even if the clergy charged with the election should be divided, the ruler is not to interfere,[33] and should renounce all "sacrilegious intrusions" on the freedom of the cathedral chapter to elect the bishop of its choice.[34] But the role of rulers in episcopal elections is not to be exclusively passive; they should strive to prevent false claimants to episcopal power from assuming or continuing to occupy the sees they covet.[35] Bernard charges all rulers to promote "in all matters the liberty of the Church."[36] The Church must be free to minister to the spiritual needs of her flock, and rulers must see to that freedom—in justice to the same people to whom they also minister. Rulers must not unjustly usurp benefices designed to support church ministries,[37] and they must not assign clerical incomes to their offspring.[38] Put more positively, the rulers of the state have the same goal as their clerical colleagues: to promote the order that allows peace and love among their people.[39]

C. Defenders of the Peace

The justice of each realm must be defended by its ruler—with force if necessary. The right ordering of the state is impossible unless rulers protect their lands from hostile invasion.[40] Like King David of old, they may be "obliged to wage war against dangerous enemies."[41] Dangerous enemies can cause internal disruption as well as violation of a state's frontiers. Rulers are also responsible for the defeat of these internal enemies; those who "divide and devastate" a country "ought to fear [the just ruler] as the protector and experience [him or her] as the avenger" of the people.[42] The terror of those "who see their land given over to depredation and plunder" must be alleviated by force of arms.[43]

It is clear that, for Bernard, warfare is sometimes necessary and, thus, can be justified. His critical concern in justifying armed action is the motivation for that action: the ruler must "choose to fight for God rather than the world."[44] Bernard writes to Abbot Suger of Saint Denis about the motivation that has sent off their king, Louis VII, to protect the Holy Land:

> He is a king who serves the King whose "kingdom endures throughout all ages [Ps 144:13]," who moves peoples and realms. Our king serves so that the King of heaven will not lose his land, the land "on which his feet have stood [Ps 131:7]." Our king—though he possesses unparalleled glory and is rich in goods, though secure in peace and victorious in battle, though still young in years—chooses to exile himself from his own lands to serve in foreign climes. Nevertheless, to serve God is to reign.[45]

To be "victorious in battle" is no vice; to battle in the service of God is a virtue.

But when is warfare in the service of God? Bernard is well aware that one can be deceived in this judgment by one's own tendencies toward aggression. He writes the people of Genoa: "If it pleases you to fight and try your courage and strength, if you would love to test your arms, by no means do so against your friends and neighbors. It would be far better for you to subdue the enemies of the Church and defend your realm against the siege and assault of the Sicilians. Over them you can prevail more sanely and more honestly, and possess what you gain with greater justice."[46] One's passion for war must be sublimated; sanity must prevail, a sanity that engages in violence only in the cause of justice, in defense of oneself and one's realm. Only when fighting in the cause of justice can one be sure one's warfare is in the service of God. Bernard writes Henry I of England: "... Justice is on our side. ... By the justice of our cause we appease God; by the force of our arms we inspire fear in the enemy...."[47] Physical violence is not intrinsically evil; it is the rulers' motivation that makes their warfare moral or immoral: "If it is never permissible for a Christian to strike with the sword, why did the Savior's precursor bid soldiers to be content with their pay [see Lk 3:14] and not forbid them to follow this calling?"[48] Armed with "religious fervor and well-disciplined behavior,... our knights show they are animated by the same zeal for the house of God which of old passionately inflamed their Leader himself when he armed his most holy hands, not indeed with a sword, but with a whip...."[49] Even in warfare the ruler should follow the example of the Lord whose flock he or she defends. In warfare, as in all of life's other pursuits, proper motivation is the key to success, the success of salvation: "The knights of Christ may safely fight the battles of the Lord, fearing neither death if they smite the enemy nor danger at their own death, since to inflict death or to die for Christ is no sin but an abundant claim to glory."[50]

For Bernard, to kill without reason is *homicidium;* to kill for good reason is *malicidium,* the killing of evil.[51] Bernard knows well that much contemporary warfare is indeed *homicidium,* for it is not fought in the just cause of self-defense. He writes the duchess of Lotharingia: "Through you I salute the duke and admonish him and you that, if you know this castle, for which you are making war, does not belong to your jurisdiction, then for God's sake leave it alone. For Scripture says: 'What will one gain if one wins the whole world [Mt 16:26],' loses oneself, 'and ruins one's life [Mk 8:36].'"[52] Unjust warfare is not only injurious to the peace of the land, it threatens the well-being of the perpetrator before God.

Louis VII of France is a target of Bernard's repeated warnings against unjust warfare:

> Do you not know how gravely you have offended [God] by forcing Count Theobald [of Champagne] to swear [an oath] against God and justice by the violence of your warfare against him?...Why do you add sin to sin [see Is 30:1] in God's presence and add, God forbid, to his anger at your behavior? How has Count Theobald sinned to merit the recurrence of your anger...? Do not, I beg you, my lord king, resist so flagrantly your King—or, rather, the creator of all— in his kingdom and in his possessions.[53]

In another letter to Louis, Bernard continues:

> From whom but the devil could the counsel come, in
> response to which you add burnings to burnings, slaughter to
> slaughter? The cries of the poor [see Ps 9:13], the sighs of the
> imprisoned [see Ps 78:11], and the blood of the slaughtered
> echo once more in the ears of the "father of orphans and the
> judge of widows [Ps 67:6]." Clearly, the ancient enemy of
> our race is delighted with this host [of victims] because "he
> was a murderer from the beginning [Jn 8:44]."[54]

Bernard extends his condemnation of unjust warfare from Louis to
all those who conduct it. In his treatise *In Praise of the New Knighthood*, he addresses the motivation for this crime, as well as the crime's
deleterious effects on the spiritual and psychological well-being of
the perpetrator:

> What, then, is the end and fruit of this worldly knighthood—
> or, rather, knavery, as I should call it? . . . Above all, there is
> that terrible insecurity of conscience, despite all your armor,
> since you have dared to undertake such dangerous warfare on
> such slight and frivolous grounds. What else moves you to
> wars and disputes except irrational flashes of anger, the thirst
> for empty glory [see Gal 5:26], or the hankering after some
> earthly possession? It is surely not safe for reasons such as
> these.[55]

Warfare, then, can be just or unjust, depending on the rulers'
motivation and the cause for which they take up arms. But violence
must be avoided whenever possible. Bernard rejoices with Empress
Rinchera over his reconciliation of the Milanese with the emperor and
the pope: "On this account I give thanks to the divine goodness who
has thus humbled your enemies without any of the dangers of war or
the shedding of human blood . . . ."[56] Whenever possible, disputes
should be settled by mediation rather than by force of arms, and
Bernard sometimes agrees to serve as mediator.[57] As Jean Leclercq has
written, Bernard "knew that violence was a fact of life whose total

abolition was not within his power; thus he tried to establish certain limits [to it] by imposing conditions as to its use and motivation."[58] Motivation is the key to both just and unjust warfare—and this key allows us to understand Bernard's own motives in preaching the Second Crusade.

D. The Crusading Servant

Behold, now is the acceptable time; behold, now is the day of abundant salvation [see 2 Cor 6:2]! "The earth has shaken and has trembled [Ps 17:8]," for the God of heaven has begun to lose his land. . . . Because of our sins, the enemies of the Cross have lifted up their sacrilegious heads, devastating with the sword that blessed land, that land of promise. Something must be done![59]

This letter to Archbishop Arnold of Cologne and Bishop Manfred of Brixen,[60] and "to all the archbishops, bishops, clergy, and people of East Frankland and Bavaria . . ."[61] is Bernard's clarion call to take the cross against those who threaten the Holy Land. Why, one must ask, does Bernard not only support but, indeed, promote warfare on the grandest scale of his time?

To be sure, Bernard knows himself commissioned to preach a new crusade by Pope Eugenius III; he writes that pope: "I rushed into this not aimlessly but at your command, or, rather, through you at God's command."[62] And the reason Bernard ascribes Eugenius's command to the will of God is that Bernard sees the crusade as a response to an unjust invasion: ". . . The Lord of heaven has begun to lose his land, . . . his land in which the voice of the turtle dove was heard [see Sg 2:12] when the Son of the Virgin called all to a pure life. . . . This promised land evil men have begun to invade . . . ."[63] The crusade is for Bernard a war of self-defense and, therefore, a war conducted in a just cause.

The religion of the invaders is not Bernard's central concern. The fact that the "evil men" who threaten the Holy Land are Muslims

—or gentiles or pagans, as Bernard alternately calls them—is not a sufficient reason to resist them: "If the gentiles were ... subject [to the rule of justice] at some future time, then I judge we should be ... patient with them rather than pursue them with swords. But, since they have instigated acts of violence against us, those who rightly bear the sword [see Rom 13:4] are obliged to drive back their forces. It is an act of Christian justice to vanquish the proud, as it is to spare the subjected...."[64] This Bernard writes to the German clergy and people. To the knights of the Temple he writes in the same vein: "I do not mean to say that the pagans are to be slaughtered when there is any other way to prevent them from harassing and persecuting the faithful. I mean only that it now seems better to strike them down than that the staff of sinners be lifted over the lot of the just [see Ps 124:3]...."[65] One should not kill Muslims because they are Muslims.[66] But Bernard sees no option other than to engage in combat with *these* Muslims, since he sees them threatening both peace and justice.[67]

Bernard looks forward to the justice that will follow the restoration of peace in the Holy Land, "when the transgressors of the divine law have been driven out...."[68] This restoration of peace and justice is a "good work."[69] It is an opportunity given by God, who could have accomplished the restoration himself but, rather, offers the task as a path to virtue to those who respond generously.[70] As Thomas Renna has written: "... It is clearly the spiritual side of the [crusading] enterprise which most interested him [Bernard]. The Muslims seem almost secondary. Bernard interiorized the holy war."[71]

But this holy war is not to be fought only to protect the peace and justice of the Holy Land. Bernard has two additional reasons for preaching the crusade. The first is that he hopes that the expedition to the East will also succeed in rescuing the Oriental Church from the Saracen threat. He writes Peter the Venerable, abbot of Cluny: "I expect that the heavy and miserable sighs of the Eastern Church have reached your ears and penetrated your heart.... If we steel our affections, if we harden our hearts, if we pay little heed to this misfortune and feel little pain at this grief, where is our love for God, where is our love for our neighbor?"[72] The same concern is obvious in a letter

Bernard writes to Suger of Saint Denis: "The Eastern Church now cries out in misery, so that whoever does not have complete compassion for her cannot be judged a true child of the Church."[73] Defense of the Church in the East is a cause that justifies warfare on her behalf.

The second of Bernard's supplemental but essential reasons for the crusade is of quite a different nature, but one completely compatible with his teaching on warfare. He writes to the clergy and people of Germany:

> Your land is well known as rich in stout men and as filled with robust youths. For this you are praised throughout the world, and the fame of your virtue fills that world. Gird yourselves manfully [see 1 M 3:58] and take up arms with joy and zeal for your Christian name. Stop your former actions—better characterized as malicious than military—by which you try to cast one another down and destroy one another, that you might eat each other up [see Gal 5:15]. Why this miserable, savage desire? The bodies of your neighbors are impaled on the sword; bodies and, perhaps, souls perish.... Stop what I see as madness not virtue, not daring but daftness. But now, O mighty soldier, O man fit for war [see 1 K 16:18], you have a place where you can fight without danger, where to win is glory "and to die is gain [Phil 1:21]."[74]

Strange as it may seem to the modern observer, Bernard preaches the crusade in the cause of peace, the peace and tranquility of a Europe that Bernard sees as bursting with the militant energies of all-too-often undiscriminating and badly motivated warriors. Bernard sends them off to the East in a cause that he considers just, and, by that action, he hopes that unjust warfare in the West will be diminished.[75]

Only the crusade which thus serves society will win success. And that service must be conducted in a spirit of fidelity and obedience or it will surely fail—as did the Second Crusade which Bernard preaches. By way of explanation of that failure, Bernard points out what he

claims the crusaders themselves acknowledge, that "they were unbe-
lieving and rebellious [see Nm 20:10]":

> ... How could they advance when they were continually
> turning back whenever they set out? And when during the
> entire journey did they not return in their hearts to Egypt
> [see Ex 16:3]? If the Israelites fell and perished because of
> their iniquity [see Ps 72:19], are we astonished that today
> those who do the same thing suffer the same fate? But was
> the destruction of the Israelites contrary to the promises of
> God? Then neither is the destruction of our men. Indeed,
> the promises of God never impair the justice of God.[76]

Bernard is intent on interiorizing the whole crusading venture, from
promising start to devastating conclusion. For him, success and failure must be measured in terms of motivation. Even military defeat
suffered in fidelity and obedience to justice can be a moral victory.[77]

This moral victory will bring reward to the generous crusader.
Bernard writes his uncle, Andrew, a knight of the Temple: "Your battle is under the sun, but in the cause of him who sits above the sun.
Here battling, there we may expect the reward. The reward for our
battle is not on earth, is not from below.... Under the sun there is
only poverty; above the sun is abundance. 'A full measure, pressed
down, shaken together, and running over, will be poured into your
lap [Lk 6:38].'"[78] To Andrew's brother Knights Templar, Bernard
repeats his injunction to be virtuous in war, for even in death they
can thereby win life:

> Go forth confidently then, you knights, and repel the foes of
> Christ's cross [see Phil 3:18] with a stalwart heart.... Rejoice,
> brave athlete, if you live and conquer in the Lord, but glory
> and exult still more if you die and join your Lord. Life is
> indeed fruitful, and victory glorious, but a holy death is more
> important than either. If "they are blessed who die in the
> Lord [Rv 14:13]," how much more are they who die for the
> Lord![79]

E. Noble Virtue

To provide peace and justice is no mean task. To accomplish their ministry, rulers must exhibit virtues of an extraordinary—one might say heroic—sort. Bernard writes to Melisande, queen of Jerusalem, on the death of her husband and her assumption of the regency of her kingdom:

> Your husband the king is dead, the little king still incapable of bearing the weight of kingly affairs and of fulfilling his royal functions. All eyes look to you, and on you alone falls the whole burden of government. You must give proof of courage and show yourself manly in your womanhood, acting in all you do with a spirit of counsel and fortitude [see Is 11:2]. You must arrange all things with prudence and moderation, so that all who see you in action may look on you more as a king than a queen. . . . But, you will say: "I am not up to that. These are weighty matters beyond my strength and ken . . . ." I know, my daughter, I know how weighty these matters are, . . . but "great is the Lord, and great is his strength [Ps 146:5]."[80]

Courage, prudence, fortitude, moderation, strength, and reliance on God's power would seem a catalogue of exceptional gifts. Yet Bernard is consistent in his high demands on the virtue of the ruler.

Bernard presents rulers models of necessary virtues in describing the Knights Templar: "I shall set forth briefly the life and virtues of the knights of Christ, for the imitation or confusion of our warriors, who, as is obvious, fight not for God but the devil . . . ."[81] Bernard's list deserves to be read in full, but even extracts demonstrate his demanding standards. Among the Templars,

> discipline is in no way lacking; obedience is never despised. . . . They shun every excess in clothing and food [see RB 29] and content themselves with what is necessary. They live as brothers in joyful and sober company. . . . They never sit in sloth or wander about aimlessly [see RB 48], but when they

are not on duty—which happens rarely—they do not eat anyone's bread without payment [see 2 Thes 3:8]; they either
repair tears in their armor or clothing, restore old equip-
ment, or set the disarranged in order. . . . There is no distinction of persons [see Rom 2:11] among them, and deference
is shown to merit rather than noble blood [see RB 63]. They
have a profound respect for one another [see Rom 12:10;
RB 72]; they bear one another's burdens and thus fulfill the
law of Christ [see Gal 6:2]. No insolent word, idle deed,
excessive laugh, not the slightest murmur or muttering is left
uncorrected once detected [see RB 4].[82]

Knights arrayed with virtues such as these are a formidable force in
battle:

When the battle is at hand, they arm themselves inwardly
with faith and outwardly with steel—and not with gold!
Thus armed, rather than decorated, they strike fear, not
excite avarice, in the enemy. They seek to have horses both
strong and swift—and not those flashily bedecked. They set
their minds on battle, not display; they seek to arouse dread,
not admiration. At the same time, they are not unruly,
impetuous, or light-mindedly rash, but soberly, prudently,
and providently draw themselves up in battle array, just as is
written of the fathers [see 2 M 12:20]. . . . They rush on their
foes . . . [but] they know not to presume on their own strength
[see Jgs 7:2], trusting for their victory in the power of the
Lord of hosts [see 2 M 15:8; Jer 11:20]. . . . Thus, in a singular and wondrous way they appear both as the mildest of
lambs and the most ferocious of lions.[83]

Bernard's catalogue of knightly virtues echoes the list of monastic
virtues described in the *Rule* of Benedict to which Bernard gave his
life-long commitment. The reminiscences of the *Rule* show this, but
Bernard is more explicit: "I do not know just what to call them [the
Templars], monks or soldiers; perhaps it would be better to recognize
them as both, for they lack neither monastic meekness nor military

might."[84] For Bernard, knightly virtues could be described in monastic terms because, in the end, monks and knights share the same goal: *human* virtue.

The fundamental virtue for all humans—monks and rulers alike—is, for Bernard, the self-knowledge of humility.[85] Rulers should recognize the good that inheres in their power and family, but they must know that their happiness does not depend on such ephemeral goods.[86] Rulers must recognize the nobility that is theirs by their human nature (*naturae ingenuitas*[87]) and put in proper perspective their nobility of birth. Virtue is a gift of God, Bernard asserts, not a gift from one's ancestors.[88] And this realization that one's virtue is a gift is an essential component of humility.

Rulers must also recognize that the success of any function of their ministry likewise requires God's gratuitous action. Bernard sends this message to the Knights Templar: "... You will not be able to keep securely and faithfully what God has entrusted to you if you trust in your own prudence and fortitude, but only if you rely totally on God's help in everything. Know 'that no one prevails by his own strength [1 Sm 2:9]....'"[89] Rulers must realistically face their own strengths and weaknesses, acknowledging that their strength is God's gift and that he will more than make up for their weaknesses.

The recognition of one's weakness will elicit love for those who are equally—though differently—weak.[90] And thus a form of loving service which Bernard repeatedly urges on rulers is care for the poor. Bernard writes Theobald of Champagne that his gifts to the poor will be accounted as love for Christ: "... Whatever it may please you in your generosity to give this servant of Christ [see Gal 1:10], you may be sure you are giving to Christ himself."[91] Gifts to God's people, and thus to God, can take many forms, but their basic need is for food, and this the ruler should freely give.[92] All the gifts of abundance that God has shared with rulers they must share with those who are needy.[93] Love is a moral imperative for all;[94] wealthy rulers can best demonstrate their loving service by caring for the needy among those to whom they minister.

The rewards for that ministry are many. Alms-giving brings the precious return of communion with the virtue of those aided. Bernard writes to Theobald of Champagne: "Help [this poor man], if not for his sake then for yours. Just as his poverty makes you necessary to him, so his holiness makes him necessary to you. Of all those whom I have sent to you, I cannot recall anyone whom I know you would please God more by helping."[95] Caring for the needy does indeed win God's favor, Bernard insists in a letter to Roger of Sicily:

> Those whom, at your word, I sent forth on their pilgrimage have been received with royal liberality. You have met them with bread [see Is 21:14], you have brought them into a place of consolation [see Ps 65:11], you have settled them on high land, the fruit of which they can eat, suck honey from the rock and oil from the hardest stone, where they might obtain butter from the herd, milk of the sheep, and figs with the kernel of wheat, and might drink the purest blood of grapes [see Dt 32:13–14]. These things are of the earth, but heavenly things can be bought with them. This is the way to the heavens; "by such sacrifices God is won [Heb 13:16]." Theirs is the kingdom of heaven [see Mt 5:3], a kingdom which will be able to return to the earthly king, living on the earth, for his earthly things, eternal life and glory.[96]

The liberality that Bernard praises in Roger must extend beyond alms-giving to all the rulers' functions.

In providing justice to their people, rulers must, of course, "love justice and hate iniquity [Ps 44:8],"[97] but they should also demonstrate a liberality which tempers the rigor of their rule. Bernard writes to the duke and duchess of Lotharingia: "Ever since I began to send into your land [for goods] to satisfy our needs, I have always found you friendly and gracious. Whenever it was needed, you have liberally bestowed the blessing of your bounty on the men we have sent. You have liberally remitted all tolls and other dues to merchants passing through your territory."[98] "Compassion and mercy"[99] should characterize rulers' administration of justice. Clemency and leniency should likewise be shown to all who hope for it.[100]

But the administration of justice calls for other virtues. To provide protection and justice, rulers must be both "vigorous in arms and agreeable in manner...."[101] The pursuit of justice and peace requires both magnanimity and strenuous action.[102] Above all, it requires the courage of Christ.[103] Defense of the peace requires rulers who are ready to "to lay down their lives for their brothers and sisters [see Jn 15:13]."[104]

Justice also demands that rulers display a courageous fidelity to the truth. Bernard writes of how well Theobald of Champagne exhibits this virtue: "For him, simply to say something is as good as an oath; the slightest untruth he regards as grave perjury."[105] Bernard continues, now speaking directly to Theobald: "Among the many signs of your virtue, which ennoble your worth and make your name celebrated throughout the world, your constancy in truth is especially praised. Who has tried to undermine, tried to weaken your firm strength by exhortation or counsel? Who, I say, has tried by guile to cast out the truth in you, a truth so holy, so profound, so worthy of imitation by all princes?"[106]

Bernard's ideal rulers match their simple honesty with external simplicity as well. Bernard's description of those who do not observe this ideal is biting:

> What then, O knights, is this monstrous error, what is this unbearable madness which bids you battle with such pomp and labor—and all to no purpose save death and crime? You bedeck your horses with silk and cover your armor with I do not know what sort of hanging bits of rag. You paint your lances, shields, and saddles. You adorn your bits and spurs with gold and silver and precious gems, and then, in all this pomp, you rush to your ruin with shameful fury and fearless folly.[107]

The honest simplicity expected of monks[108] is the standard for rulers as well.

Rulers, then, should be simple ministers to their people. They must exhibit heroic virtues to bring their people the peace and justice that will enable them to flourish before God. Bernard's admonition to the newly widowed Queen Melisande is an eloquent summation of this teaching:

Before God you are a widow, before your people a queen. Consider the queen whose worthy or unworthy deeds cannot be hidden under a bushel basket, but are set up high on a candelabrum, that they may be apparent to all [see Mt 5:15]. Consider the widow whose concern is no longer to please her husband [see 1 Cor 7:34] but solely to be able to please God. Blessed are you if you make the Savior a wall [see Is 26:1] for the protection of your conscience, a breastwork to ward off disgrace. Blessed are you, I say, if, alone and a widow [see 1 Tm 5:5], you give yourself wholly to God's rule. For unless you are well ruled, you will not rule well.[109]

In Bernard's eyes, peace and justice on earth can be obtained and maintained only through the actions of lay rulers like Melisande, whose virtue makes them worthy ministers to God's folk.

VII

The Dissidents

There were some inhabitants of the early twelfth-century world who did not fit easily into Bernard's view of society, into his ecclesiology, because they did not share the prevailing Christian views of Western Europeans. These were schismatics, heretics, pagans, Jews, and Muslims. But Bernard does not exclude them from his view of society—nor does he exclude them from the possibility of salvation. Bernard perceives that the Church "prays confidently for Jews, for heretics, and for pagans."[1]

Bernard writes Eugenius III of his sorrow over the schismatic Eastern Church, over "the obstinacy of the Greeks, who are both with us and not with us. Joined in faith with us, they are separated from harmony with us. Even in matters of the faith itself, they have lamely wandered from the right paths [see Ps 17:46]."[2] Although Bernard believes "God is indeed angry with schismatics...," he finds God "no more pleased with Catholics."[3] Bernard's response to schism is twofold: correction[4] and concern and care for the schismatics' welfare—even to launching a crusade on their behalf.[5]

A. Heretics and Pagans

Heretics are more serious problem.[6] The schismatic Greeks are removed geographically; heretics present an internal threat to the faith of Bernard's Church. He writes Hildefons, count of Saint Gilles and Toulouse, of the danger posed by the preaching of Henry of Lausanne:

How often have I heard of and recognized [see Ps 77:3] the
evils being done in the Church of God, done each day by the
heretic Henry. He dwells in your land, a rapacious wolf in
sheep's clothing [see Mt 7:15]. But, as the Lord has pointed
out, by his fruits we can know him [see Mt 7:16]: churches
without people, people without priests, priests without due
reverence, and Christians without Christ. The churches are
regarded as synagogues, the sanctuary of God is denied holiness, the sacraments are not considered sacred, the holy days
are deprived of solemnities. People die in their sins [see Jn
8:24]; alas, souls are everywhere snatched before the terrible
tribunal unreconciled by penance and unsupported by holy
Communion.[7]

Bernard is incensed at the treatment he sees children receiving from
Henry and his fellow heretics:

The life of Christ is shut off from Christian children, for the
grace of Baptism is denied. They are turned away from
approaching their salvation despite the Savior's affectionate
cry for them: "Let the little children come to me [Mk 10:
14]." Does God, who keeps folk and beast, who multiplies
his mercy to them [see Ps 35:7–8], deny his manifold mercy
only to the innocent? Why deny children the Savior-child who
was born for them [see Is 9:6]? This is diabolical envy; "by this
envy death came into the world [see Ws 2:24]." Or does this
man think the Savior does not desire children because they are
children? If this is the case, then it was for nothing that the
great Lord was made small—to say nothing of being scourged,
spat upon, crucified, and put to death.[8]

Heresy is, for Bernard, an attack both on social order and on the
well-being of God's people who benefit from that order.

How would Bernard handle heresy? First, by refutation, "for an
error publicly refuted does not spring up again, and falsehood revealed
does not take root."[9] This is the task of the clergy.[10] Unrepentant

heretics are "most justly turned out of the Church to which they have caused scandal...."[11] But heretics must not be attacked physically, as has been done: "People have attacked them, making new martyrs for the cause of their godless heresy. I approve their zeal, but I do not advocate their action. For faith should be a matter of persuasion, not of imposition."[12] Bernard does allow temporal rulers to protect society from attack when the behavior of the heretics disturbs public order[13]—for example, by public cohabitation of the unmarried.[14] But the ultimate goal should be the conversion and reconciliation of the heretic: "... Heretics are to be caught rather than driven away. They are to be caught, I repeat, not by force of arms but by arguments through which their errors may be refuted. If possible, they themselves should be reconciled with Catholics and called back to the true faith. This is his [God's] will [see Jn 6:39–40]: 'He wants all folk saved and brought to knowledge of the truth [1 Tm 2:4].'"[15] Bernard wishes the salvation, not the annihilation, of the heretic.

This irenicism seems flatly contradicted by the attitude toward pagans reflected in Bernard's letter to the crusaders about to attack the Wends. Bernard writes: "I forbid you to enter into a treaty with them—in any way or for any reason whatsoever: not for money, not for tribute, until, by God's help, either their religious observances or their nation be destroyed."[16] But Bernard issues this admonition in the context of a crusade to the Holy Land, not one directed against the Wends. He fears the Wends will attack the line of march to the East and thus "close the road to Jerusalem...." The "conversion of the nations" is Bernard's first concern; only if the Wends unjustly attack those who have "taken the sign of salvation" should they, in turn, be attacked.[17]

The reason for Bernard's vehemence is not the Wends' paganism but their anticipated assault on a just cause. As Jean Leclercq writes: "... Bernard believed it necessary first to dominate them by force, not in order to convert them by this means, which he declared illegitimate, but to prevent them from jeopardizing Christians."[18] Bernard does indeed hope for the conversion of pagans, whom he sees as a vineyard to be cultivated by Christians.[19] But the motive of the pagans in converting should be a love that comes from their realization of God's love for them: "Easily do they love more who recognize they are loved more.... [Pagans,] ... who are not spurred on by such a love as the Church experiences ... ,"[20] must be evangelized[21] not eliminated.

B. MUSLIMS AND JEWS

The same principles are even more obvious in Bernard's teaching on Muslims. As we have seen,[22] Bernard does not preach a crusade against Muslims, but rather a war of self-defense against "evil men" who are unjustly threatening peace and security in the East. The fact that the invaders are Muslims is not Bernard's concern. Were they just, they should be tolerated.

Bernard's teaching on Jews is a different matter, for the situation of Jews in medieval Europe is quite different. They are indeed *in* Europe, not an external threat. Bernard's response to the Jewish presence seems ambivalent. In his *Fourteenth Sermon on the Song of Songs,* for example, he rejoices in Israel's privileged position in God's salvific plan but condemns Jewish rejection of the keystone of that plan[23] and its universal applicability:

> ... The synagogue stood in the way [of early Christians], insisting that a church gathered from among the gentiles would be unclean and unworthy.... You, [O Synagogue,] will be abandoned to your blind and contentious error until the gentile multitudes, which you proudly spurn and enviously reject, shall have entered the fold [see Rom 11:25] and until you have acknowledged him who is renowned in Judea and whose name is great in Israel [see Ps 75:2].... But God will not cast them off forever [see Ps 43:23].... Mindful of his mercy, he will receive Israel his child [see Lk 1:54], so that mercy will be a companion to judgment....[24]

There are indeed negative elements here—but there is also confidence in the ultimate salvation of Jews. This is why

> the Jews must not be persecuted, slain, or cast out. Ask those who know the divine pages what they read prophesized in

the psalm about the Jews; the Church says: "He [God] will disclose me above my enemies; do not kill them, lest my people ever forget [Ps 58:12]." ... They are dispersed; they are entrusted to others; they endure a hard captivity under Christian princes.... But, when the full number of the gentiles have entered in, then all Israel will be saved, as the apostle says [in Rom 11:25–26].... If the Jews are utterly destroyed, what will become of our hope for their promised salvation, for their eventual conversion?[25]

That conversion is God's work and will be accomplished in his own good time. Churchmen are to wait on God's pleasure and not attempt to convert Jews: "Time excuses you," he writes to the pope, "in the case of the Jews; they have their end which cannot be anticipated. The full number of the gentiles must come in first [see Rom 11:25]."[26] Gratitude, not attempts at conversion, is the duty of the Church toward Jews:

Let not the branches be ungrateful to the root, nor children to their mother. Let not the branches grudge the roots the sap they took from them; let not children grudge their mother the milk they sucked from her breasts. Let the Church hold fast to the salvation which the Jews lost. She holds it fast until the full measure of the gentiles comes in, and then all Israel will be saved [see Rom 11:25–26]. Let her wish that universal salvation might come to all, for it can be possessed by all without anyone having less. The Church does wish this—and more. For she desires for the Jews the name and grace of a bride, and this is more than salvation.[27]

Anyone who could write this "astonishing passage"[28] could not condone the persecution of Jews. To the contrary, Bernard says, those who preach persecution "approve of the freedom to murder."[29] Persecution is "the foulest heresy, a sacrilegious prostitution, impregnated by the spirit of lies; it is 'conceived in sorrow and gives birth to injustice [Ps 7:15].'"[30] Christians must not persecute Jews; otherwise "what becomes of the saying: 'The Lord builds up Jerusalem; he will gather together the scattered children of Israel [Ps 146:2]'?"[31]

Bernard's ecclesiology is comprehensive. His view of the Church and of society includes a sophisticated and splendidly thorough analysis of the functions and virtues of monks, clerics, and lay folk. And he does not neglect those whose theological positions or ecclesial status put them outside of the mainstream of Western and Christian society. His views on dissidence are remarkably irenic: he wishes all dissidents the happiness of salvation and, thus, exalted participation in a new and heavenly society.

VIII

Daniel, Noah, and Job: A Hierarchy?

ernard's clear distinction between the various classes and callings is obvious in his image of Noah, Daniel, and Job, each crossing safely the sea of life on the journey to happiness in this world and the next. Monks, clergy, and lay folk are all recipients of God's loving care and, thus, capable of producing people of heroic virtue. Each calling follows its own rule of life, and each of these can bring the riches of perfection. The various orders of the Church and society are united in their diversity, all having the same goal and supporting one another in the pursuit of that goal. Whatever calling the individual member of one or another order receives, Bernard is confident that the person who responds with loving generosity will receive the reward of heavenly happiness.[1]

But this summary leaves unasked an important question: Are there some vocations which are intrinsically more efficacious in the pursuit of happiness? To put the question another way: Are there some ways of life more suitable to the perfection of the human being? There is surely some evidence that Bernard valued the life of the monk as better in itself than the life of the clergy and laity living in the world. Hugh Feiss has written that, for Bernard, "men of the monastic profession choose a more secure way of life; they seem to be the brightest members of the bright body of the Church. They lack the distraction of earthly cares."[2] Feiss points out that the "daily baptism of a life of penitence ... seems [for Bernard] practically impossible in the world; hence, those who wish to live repentantly should enter a strict monastery."[3]

Bernard's letter to the brother of William, one of the monks of Clairvaux, seems to support the notion that Bernard saw the monastic life as superior to even a virtuous life in the world:

> I wish you to be a friend of the poor, but I should prefer that you be their imitator. The former is the stage of the proficient, the latter of the perfect. Friendship for the poor makes us the friend of kings; love of poverty makes us kings ourselves. . . . You see how great is the dignity of holy poverty. . . . This [poverty] which, without human or angelic aid, simply with confidence in divine gifts, approaches the face of glory, lays hold of the highest things, reaches the summit of all splendor.[4]

Poverty—presumably, that of the monk—is superior to the care for the poor that William's brother might meritoriously demonstrate as a man living in the world—so this text seems to say. Another text—this time in Bernard's treatise on the Templars—would seem to say something similar. Bernard writes of the soldier's calling that it is "permitted," provided that one has not embraced a "higher calling."[5] This notion of a "higher calling" led me, at one time, to write of Bernard's social thought: "Thus, although the states of life were all good [for Bernard], there was an ethical factor which established them in a hierarchical relationship."[6] Further study has led me to believe that this statement confuses the question and does not do justice to Bernard's thought.

There are two reasons for this, and the first is a more complete understanding of Bernard's anthropology. As I wrote in *The Spiritual Teachings of Bernard of Clairvaux*: "Over the past several years, I have become more and more convinced that the key to understanding the spirituality of Bernard of Clairvaux, the spirituality of the twelfth century, indeed, the spirituality of any person or age, is anthropology. The completion—the self-fulfillment, the happiness—of human beings necessarily depends on what human beings are."[7] The central concern in applying this principle to a supposedly bernardine social hierarchy is Bernard's attitude toward the body. If Bernard were hostile to the human body and, consequently, to things of the "flesh," then a hierarchical social structure would inevitably emerge. If one reads Bernard as if he were a neo-platonist—albeit a Christian neo-platonist—then the anthropology that results sees the human body—and all things physical—as one step above non-being and immeasurably inferior to the human soul and spiritual substance. The social theory that results from such a reading is then equally neo-platonic: the greater a social group's involvement in the things of this world, in material things, the lower is that group's status in such a social hierarchy. Monks, being spiritual, are at the summit of such a hierarchy; clergy, active in the world, are less "spiritual" and hence assume a lower position; lay folk, heavily involved in the cares of the world and permitted the physical act of procreation, occupy the lowest rank. The life of people in the world then becomes "worldly life."[8]

But this will not work. At times Bernard does indeed have some apparently harsh things to say of the body, referring to it on one occasion as "almost bestial."[9] But Bernard's teaching on the body is not so simple, and what emerges from a study of his many texts on the matter[10] is an overwhelmingly positive attitude toward human beings and their bodies. Bernard writes: "In both body and soul the human being is the most admirable of all creatures, the body and soul being united by the incomprehensible ingenuity and unsearchable wisdom [see Rom 11:33] of the Creator."[11] Without the body, Bernard is sure, the happiness of the beatific vision is inaccessible to the human being.[12] Bernard's anthropology is not neo-platonic, and so his social theory is likewise not susceptible to a neo-platonic interpretation.

A. THE HIERARCHY OF VIRTUE

The second reason for rejecting my earlier assessment of Bernard's supposedly hierarchical social theory lies in a development of my "happy fault" in ascribing to this part of Bernard's thought "an ethical factor."[13] There is indeed a hierarchical evaluation within Bernard's teaching on vocations, but it is not a hierarchy based on the worthiness of the social class but on the response of the individual to her or his calling—whatever that calling may be.

It is on the basis of virtue, not calling, that God assigns rooms in his heavenly house:

> The Church's expectation, founded on the death of Christ, is joyful and undoubting. . . . How gladly she mentally visits those clefts [in the rock; see Sg 2:14] through which the ransom of his sacred blood flowed upon her! How gladly she explores the crannies, the refreshing retreats and rooms, which are so many and so diverse in the Father's house [see Jn 14:2], in which he places his children according to the diverse merits of each![14]

The merits and their rewards are diverse, as are the vocations of those rewarded "because they live according to their own laws within the Church. . . . Noah, Daniel, and Job each have a share in the one kingdom . . . [though] they do not follow the same path of justice."[15]

There is indeed a hierarchy in Bernard's social thought, in his ecclesiology. It is a hierarchy not of classes but of individuals; it is a hierarchy based not on the worthiness of the class to which one belongs but on one's response to the moral responsibilities of one's class. One's status in Bernard's eyes is a function of one's response to the challenges of life—whatever the calling to which one is called.[16] Bernard's moral hierarchy is based on one's conformity to the demands of one's station in life:

> There are some acts which are glorious but which can be omitted without fault. . . . Not to touch a woman [see 1 Cor 7:1] is no little virtue [for a monk], but there is no fault if married persons embrace their own spouses. Of this sort are all the evangelical counsels about which it can be appropriately said: "Let anyone accept this who can [Mt 19:12]." On the other hand, there are some acts the neglect of which is a blunder, but which bring no special glory to those who do them. Then there are those acts which one scorns at one's peril but bring no glory to their authors.[17]

Some acts, then, are useful, some are necessary, some are permissible —or even virtuous—depending one one's state of life.

It is not one's state of life that is more or less spiritual, it is one's response to that state and one's moral judgments within it:

> The spiritual person...must always precede each undertaking with a three-fold consideration: first, whether it is lawful; second, whether it is suitable; last, whether it is also advantageous [see 1 Cor 6:12, 10:22]. Even if it can be established surely by means of Christian wisdom that nothing is suitable unless it is lawful, and that nothing is advantageous unless it is suitable and lawful, it does not necessarily follow that all that is lawful will be suitable or advantageous.[18]

Bernard's teaching obviously brings both a wide-ranging freedom and a concomitant responsibility to the individual. Bernard offers guidelines in the exercise of that burden of freedom: "...One must know that some things are completely good, others completely evil. In these obedience is due to no one, for the former may not be omitted even when prohibited, the latter cannot be done even when commanded. Between these extremes, there is an intermediate class of actions which can be good or bad, depending on circumstances of manner, place, time, or person...."[19] Some actions are clearly wrong or right. But for many actions, the choice is not so obvious. In the discernment[20] necessary to virtuous choice and action in these matters, one should be guided by one's ministry in the Church, by one's social responsibilities as a monk, cleric, or lay person:

> ...There is an intermediate class of actions which we recognize as neither good nor evil in themselves. These can be indifferently, either well or ill, commanded or forbidden, and it is never evil to obey in such matters. As examples I offer fasting, vigils, meditative reading, and the like. But you must know that many intermediate actions can be transformed into matters purely good or evil. Thus marriage, which can be legitimately entered into or avoided, must not be dissolved

once contracted. What, therefore, before the nuptials was clearly an intermediate action, becomes a virtue wholly good for married persons. Likewise, to possess property—or not to possess it—is an intermediate matter for persons living in the world, but for monks, who may not possess property, it is a matter wholly evil.[21]

Many, if not most, actions are neither virtuous nor vicious in themselves. Virtue depends on the circumstances and a good intention in choosing the action contemplated: "What proceeds from a pure heart and a good conscience [see 1 Tm 1:5] is virtue, white and shining. And, if it is followed by a good reputation, it is a lily too, for it has both color and fragrance."[22]

The fundamental virtues are the same for all classes of people. The most basic of these is the intellectual virtue of self-knowledge, which Bernard calls humility.[23] This self-knowledge must include a recognition that one's social status is no indication of virtue.[24] Neither clerics nor monks are immune to the potential self-deception of status consciousness.[25] The measure of the virtue or vice of each member of all social groups is not the status that their class confers, but the recognition of who and what they are—and the choice or rejection of the responsibilities of their ministry.

Whatever his or her calling, each person must respond to it in love. All share the need for the intellectual virtue of self-knowledge; all share the need for the volitional virtue of love:

Show me a soul who loves nothing but God and what is to be loved for God's sake, to whom to live is Christ [see Ps 15:8], and of whom this has long been true. Show me a soul who, in work and leisure alike, endeavors to keep God always before her eyes and tries to walk with the Lord her God [see Mi 6:8], with a will not merely generous but single-minded, and who does so at every opportunity. Show me, I say, such a soul, and I shall not deny she is worthy of the Bridegroom's care, of the regard of his majesty, of his sovereign favor, of his solicitous guidance . . . .[26]

The happiness of perfection is open to all who lead a virtuous life of humility and love: "At all times and for all persons...care [for the virtues] brings salvation."[27] And the happiness of perfection is not reserved to the next life, because, for Bernard, perfection is a process, not a conclusion: "Unwearied effort at progress, unflagging effort to be perfect, is accounted perfection."[28] Regardless of the social class to which one belongs, Bernard is confident that a loving response to God's love will lead one to the goal of happiness.[29]

B. The "Highest" Calling

Still, there are a number of passages in Bernard's works that would seem to fit with difficulty—if, indeed, they can be made to fit at all—into Bernard's view of society as a variety of parallel occupations, vocations, or ministries. If, for example, lay folk, clerics, and monks follow parallel, though distinct, paths to perfection, how does one deal with Bernard's many admonitions to leave the world and come to the cloister? To Romanus, a subdeacon in the Roman curia, Bernard writes: "Make haste, go forth, depart!...Flee [the world], I implore you; do not remain standing in the path of sinners [see Ps 1:1]! How can you live where you would not dare to die?"[30] This surely seems an indictment of life in the world, but the context of the quotation indicates that Romanus has long promised to embrace the monastic life and that Bernard is exercising his rhetorical skills to confirm the cleric in that decision. Bernard's letter to Geoffry of Lisieux is, perhaps, still more vehement in urging the life of the cloister, but it is also quite clear from the letter that Geoffry has promised himself to the monastery and then withdrawn at the advice of those close to him.[31]

But Bernard does not always insist on the fulfillment of a promise to become a monk. His letter to William, count of Nevers, indicates that there can be good reasons for postponing such a promised conversion of life style: "Since you assure me that present needs, compassion for the poor, and the cares undertaken by your household seem to forbid for now your coming to the cloister, I too, in so far as it rests with me, will not keep you away from what love speaks to you—

provided that you do not tarry beyond the time you have yourself determined."[32] This is a letter of support for an individual; it is clearly not intended to denigrate the virtues of life in the world.

In the some fourteen of Bernard's letters counseling entrance into the monastery, the dominant motif is the welfare of the individual and the fulfillment of the personal needs of the aspirant.[33] Two of these letters support the aspirants' perceived monastic call, but Bernard counsels against Cistercian life, which he thinks too demanding physically for them.[34] Bernard sends another aspirant away from Clairvaux to a daughter house closer to the young man's home.[35] In another letter, Bernard reassures the parents of one aspirant that their son is capable of Cistercian life and that Bernard will watch carefully to see this is so.[36] The great bulk of Bernard's letters encouraging young folk to embrace monastic life, some nine of them, are directed to those who have promised to come or have clearly indicated that they wish to do so.[37] Only one of the "recruitment letters" contains no reference to the previous intention of the aspirant, but Bernard clearly thinks the monastic life would be better for him than the life he is leading.[38] In these letters, Bernard's intention is not to elaborate a hierarchy of social classes culminating in the monastic calling. He wishes to aid individuals in the pursuit of a life that will help them achieve their own perfection.

1. The Sermon on Conversion

Bernard's sermon to the clergy of Paris (usually called *On Conversion*) has often been seen as an expression of his deep conviction that the monastic life is in itself superior to all other callings. The sermon has also been taken as a monastic assault on the clerical status and the life associated with it.[39]

One of Bernard's biographers, Geoffry of Auxerre, was present when Bernard delivered the sermon, and Geoffry has left the following account:

> Once it happened that the man of God traveled to parts of
> Gaul on business. Both on his way and return, he preached a

sermon on conversion, as he often did, to the students of Paris. That evening he began to sorrow and be fearful, saying to God in prayer: "I greatly fear that you have forgotten me completely because, contrary to the usual pattern, my trip has been utterly fruitless, and no door has opened for me [see 1 Cor 16:9] in speaking your word to these clerics." But, at that very hour God so consoled him that he foresaw plainly and predicted: "I shall not go away empty-handed from this place."[40]

Geoffry tells us that his conversion—and that of many others—was accomplished on that day:

Blessed be that day, on which the Sun of justice—rather, of mercy—arose and shown from on high [see Lk 1:78] on my poor soul. And an exceedingly adverse and perverse man—in one word, in one moment, in the twinkling of an eye [see 1 Cor 15:52]—was re-created into a completely new man by the right hand of the Most High [see Ps 76:11], so that I might begin to be his creature [see Jas 1:18]. I shall never forget his loving-kindness [see Ps 118:93] in moving me by the flood of his prevenient grace and changing me so suddenly that many were astounded at me. Truly, many fish were caught in the nets of the Lord in that catch . . . so that, after our year of probation, there were twenty-one of our band who would become monks.[41]

Does Geoffry's account match Bernard's motivation? If so, then it would seem that Bernard's efforts to convert the clerics of Paris is a reflection of a hierarchical approach to the various callings in the Church. The best source for Bernard's intention is, of course, his sermon.

Bernard's criticism of Parisian students is harsh indeed: "No one deserves greater wrath than the enemy simulating friendship, 'Judas, you betray the Son of man with a kiss [Lk 22:48].' You, a familiar friend, who took sweet foods with him [see Ps 54:14–15], who have dipped your hand in the same small dish [see Mt 26:23]! You have no share in the prayer he prayed to his Father: 'Father, forgive them, for they do not know what they do [Lk 23:34].'"[42] Bernard's devastating condemnation is based on his perception that the members of his audience have betrayed their own calling: "Woe to you who have appropriated a path not only of knowledge but also of authority. . . . You have taken, not received, the keys."[43] And it is by their ambition that the Paris scholars show themselves unfaithful to their clerical way of life: "Whence this great ardor for a prelacy? Whence such ambitious impudence? Whence such madness of human presumption? Would anyone who did not teach but hinder our secular laws dare to occupy a ministry, snatch its income, and regulate its affairs?"[44] Bernard contrasts this ambition with the virtues demanded of the clerical vocation: purity of heart, a commitment to peacemaking, and love for the flock. Bernard condemns those unfaithful ministers, those "children of wrath," who "are found in the business of reconciling others . . . when they themselves are not reconciled." He condemns "those walking in the flesh, . . . [who] cannot please God and yet presume to please."[45] This is indeed a powerful condemnation of Bernard's clerical audience, but it is in no sense a criticism of the clerical ministry.

It is, rather, an indictment of those who hold—or hope to hold—the clerical office for unworthy reasons or who live a life unworthy of their calling:

> Everywhere they rush into holy orders. Without awe, without thought, they appropriate to themselves a ministry which awes angelic spirits. . . . In them avarice rules, ambition commands, pride dominates, iniquity is in the saddle, luxury is lord. Were we to dig within their walls. . . . we might well find the worst abomination [see Ez 8:8–10], we might well see a horror in the house of God. Beyond fornication, beyond adultery [see 1 Cor 6:9], beyond incest [see 1 Cor 5:1], there are some among them who have given themselves up to disgraceful passions and shameful acts [see Rom 1:26].[46]

Bernard's sermon is indeed an attempt to convert the clergy, not to the monastic life, but rather to a way of life that will make them capable of filling—and finding fulfillment in—their own office and ministry. Bernard's clerical hearers have been unfaithful to their vocation to the active ministry—they have also been unfaithful to their calling to be humans[47]—and Bernard calls them to conversion to a worthy ministry and a truly human life.

Still, one passage in Bernard's sermon could be considered an effort to recruit his audience to the monastic way of life. Bernard pleads:

> Spare, I beg you, my brothers, spare your souls; spare the blood which has been poured out for you [see Mt 26:28]. Beware the terrible danger; turn away from the fire which has been prepared [see Mt 25:41].... Is not chastity put in peril amid delights, humility amid riches, justice amid much business, truth amid much talk, love in this present world [see Gal 1:4]? Flee from the midst of Babylon [see Jer 51:6]! Flee and save your souls [see Jer 48:6]! Flock to the cities of refuge [see Jos 21:36] where you can do penance for the past, obtain grace for the present, and confidently await future glory.[48]

If the "cities of refuge" are meant to be monasteries, then perhaps this passage might be taken as an invitation to flee the world for the cloister. I do not think so, for the context does not mention monasteries.

Even were this Bernard's meaning, it could be taken as an extension of the principle Bernard proposes in a letter to Thurstan, the archbishop of York. Thurstan has expressed his desire to become a monk; Bernard admonishes him against this change of vocation:

> I praise your desire for quiet and your desire to fall asleep peacefully in the Lord [see Ac 7:59]. But the reasons you offer do not seem sufficient to abandon your pastoral care, unless—which God forbid and I do not believe—you have committed some grave deed, or you have obtained permission to do as you wish by the authority of the pope. I do not believe you are ignorant of the words of the apostle: "Are you bound to a wife? Do not seek to be loosed [1 Cor 7:27]."

> The promise which you say you have made is not binding
> on a bishop, one called to continue steadfastly in the min-
> istry to which he has been called. Without prejudice to the
> opinions of those wiser than I, it seems better to me that
> you should hold on to what you now hold [see 2 Thes 2:7]
> and exhibit in a bishop the habit of humility and a monastic
> life and holiness.[49]

Thurstan can abandon his clerical ministry, as Bernard sees it, only with
the permission of a higher authority or because of some serious fault.

In Bernard's sermon to the clerics of Paris there is no mention of
permission, but Bernard clearly sees in his audience grave fault that
would justify an abandonment, by at least some of them, of their
clerical status.[50] This whole sermon/treatise *On Conversion* shows Bernard's great respect for the clerical ministry and contains no degrada-
tion of it in favor of a monastic vocation. The clerical ministry is so
precious that its aspirants must convert to a way of life that will fit
them for it. Those who cannot live up to its rigorous demands should
abandon their ambition to minister in this way. But Bernard does not
urge them to come to the cloister. Conversion is a gift open to all
sinful human beings; it surely does not necessarily mean entry into a
monastery.[51]

2. Cluniacs and Cistercians

One of Bernard's letters to Geoffry, abbot of the Benedictine monastery of Saint Mary in York, contains this apparently belligerent
passage:

> That your brothers have left you has been done without the
> knowledge, counsel, or encouragement of myself or of my
> monks.... Pope Saint Gregory writes in his book, *Pastoral
> Care* [1.27]: "Whoever undertakes a greater good and deter-
> mines to do a lesser good, does the unlawful." ... In his third
> homily on Ezekiel [1.3.18], Gregory writes in the same vein:
> "There are some who do the good they have vowed and, in

the midst of this action, decide on a better. But then they change their minds and retract the better intentions on which they have decided. They do the good they have begun, but they surrender the better which they have decided to do. These persons appear quite just in human eyes, but, in the eyes of the omnipotent God, they have fallen away from their resolution."[52]

Bernard seems to imply that not all monasteries are created equal and that transfer[53] from the inferior to the superior is demanded of those who recognize the distinction. If this is so, how can one avoid concluding that Bernard's attitude in this matter is inconsistent with his profession of parallel callings in the Church? If there is a hierarchy of monastic vocations, how can this be consistent with his affirmation that virtue, not status, is the ultimate criterion in judging human lives? Bernard's relationship with contemporary Cluniac monasticism may provide answers to these questions.[54]

One important source regarding this relationship is Bernard's letter to his nephew Robert, who has exchanged Cistercian life for that of the Cluniacs. In that letter Bernard delivers a stinging description of the life Robert has chosen:

Does salvation consist more in opulent dress and food than in frugal fare and moderate clothing? If soft and warm furs, if fine and precious cloth, if long sleeves and ample hoods, if silvan covers and soft threads make a saint, why should I delay and not follow you? But these are mitigations for the weak not the armor of warriors. "Behold, those clothed in soft garments are in the houses of kings [Mt 11:8]." Wine and white bread, mead and heavy wine, serve the body not the spirit. The soul is not fattened out of frying pans, but the body is. There were many brothers in [the deserts of] Egypt who long served God without fish. Pepper, ginger, cumin, sage, and a thousand of these sorts of spices may please the palate, but they inflame inordinate desire. Would you place me in this sort of security? Would you cheat a youth with this sort of tutor?[55]

What Robert has done is "without a doubt to look back, walk crookedly, and apostatize."[56] Is Robert's apostasy a choice of an inferior way of life or a failure to live up to his own potential for virtue? Or, perhaps, both?

Bernard's *Apology to Abbot William* is surely his most noted commentary on Cluniac life. His descriptions are devastating:

> I am astonished that among monks there could arise such intemperance in food and drink, in clothing and bedding, in riding equipment and building construction. It has come to the point that the more these concerns, delights, and extravagances are cultivated, the better right order is said to be promoted, the greater holiness is thought to be. Behold, frugality is thought to be avarice, sobriety is believed to be austerity, silence is considered to be sadness. But laxity is viewed as discretion, extravagance as generosity, loquacity as affability, immoderate laughter as agreeability. Soft clothing and haughty horses are said to be respectable, superfluous bedding to be care for cleanliness. When we lavish these on others, it is called love. Such love destroys love; this discretion confounds discretion. Such kindness is full of cruelty, for it so serves the body that the soul is strangled.[57]

This is surely satire, and, as Jean Leclercq has written, "the exaggerations to be found in the *Apologia* were no more than one would expect to find in a satire; both Bernard and his readers understood this.... The *Apologia* is not a factual document meant to convey details of the actual state of Cluniac observance. It is a caricature, designed to correct them."[58] Peter the Venerable's satire on the cookery at his own monastery of Cluny was as biting as Bernard's.[59] For both Bernard and Peter, their satire was "really meant to help the forces of reform within the great Cluniac family."[60] But does Bernard's satire also aim at establishing the *in se* superiority of Cistercian life? Does it also affirm a hierarchy not simply of virtue but also of status?

The *Apology* offers a seemingly ambivalent answer. Even an attempt by Bernard to mitigate the severity of his attack contains some evidence of a hierarchical approach to monastic states of life:

> If only the stricter would cease their criticism and the more
> remiss would pare away the superfluous.... If only the per-
> son who takes to himself the good would not envy the bet-
> ter, and the one who is seen to pursue a better course would
> not spurn the good of the other.... Just as it is not legitimate
> for those who have vowed the greater to descend to the
> lesser—lest they apostatize—so it is not fitting for all who do
> the lesser good to go over to the practice of the greater—lest
> they be overcome.[61]

Despite the evaluation of some lifestyles as greater or better, and
some as lesser or simply good, Bernard's concern is, in the last analysis, with the appropriateness of the lifestyle to the physical, psychological, and spiritual needs of the individual. There is ample evidence
of this, both in the *Apology* and elsewhere. In the *Apology,* Bernard
writes:

> I am myself a Cistercian; do I therefore condemn the Cluni-
> acs? God forbid! On the contrary, I love them, praise them,
> extol them.... If you ask why...I did not choose Cluny from
> the first, I reply that, as the apostle says...: "All things are
> lawful for me, but all things are not profitable for me [1 Cor
> 10:22]." It is not that Cluny is not holy and just. It is rather
> that I am an unspiritual man, sold as a slave to sin [see Rom
> 7:14]. I knew that my soul was so weak that a stronger remedy
> was necessary. Different diseases call for different remedies; the
> more serious the illness, the more drastic the remedy.[62]

Bernard chooses the Cistercian life because its strict observance of
the *Rule* is more suitable to his personal needs than other monastic
paths to perfection.

And Bernard counsels the same for others as well. Responding to
Abbot Hildegarius and the brothers of the Benedictine monastery of
Flay, who have complained at the reception of one of their number at
Clairvaux, Bernard writes: "If one of our monks should hasten to
you, desiring the grace of greater perfection and a stricter life, not

only should we not dispute your counseling him in his endeavor, we should beg you sincerely to do so. We should not complain of offense but recognize you as great benefactors."[63]

Given Bernard's teaching that it is God who provides a way of life to each person, a life in accord with each person's needs, Bernard sometimes supports an individual's transfer to a more rigorous life: "... Often the attempt to lead a more austere life has a soothing effect on anxious souls for whom the state of life to which they have been committed was not sufficient."[64] But Bernard directs others to a less rigorous life when they seem more suited to it. He writes to William, abbot of the canons regular at Troyes: "I have persuaded this cleric, who desires to leave the world and remain with us, to come instead to your order, fearing that the difficulties of our life would break him. I should like to keep him because of his virtuous life, but I fear receiving him because he is a delicate man, unused to manual labor."[65] Bernard sends two other young men to a Benedictine community for the same reason: "These two young men have good wills but not the physical strength necessary for life in my order. Therefore, I am sending them to you...."[66] If the spiritual, psychological, and physical needs of those who apply for admission to Clairvaux are better suited to life elsewhere, Bernard refuses to accept them.[67] He also dissuades many from leaving their own monastery for Clairvaux and sends them back if they decamp to his cloister.[68]

Whether going or staying, the needs of the individual are paramount. To Simon, who has encountered difficulties in an attempt to introduce a more rigorous life into his Benedictine abbey in the diocese of Laon, Saint Nicolas-aux-Bois, Bernard writes:

I would counsel you, venerable father, to moderate for now the rigors proposed by you and those of the same mind. And this, so that you do not neglect the welfare of the weak. Those in the order of Cluny whom you have consented to rule should be invited, not driven, to a stricter way of life. Those who desire to live on a loftier plane should be persuaded to accommodate themselves to the weaker out of love for them—as much as they can without sin. Or those who wish to hold to a stricter way of life could be permitted to do so—if that can be done without scandal to either group. Or, if it is necessary, those who desire to live according to your proposals could be set free from your congregation to join other communities.[69]

A more rigorous way of life may not be what one needs, and, in such cases, Bernard adamantly advises against seeking such a way. He writes to a Benedictine nun of Saint Mary's near Troyes:

I have been told you wish to leave your monastery under the pretext of seeking a more austere life.... But I do not see how, given your understanding of the matter, your desire can be implemented in any way. Do you ask why? Is it not wise for me to flee opulence, frequent visits to town, and rich, delicious food? Would not my virtue be better protected in a wilderness where I could live in peace, either alone or with a few others, pleasing him alone whom I have accepted [see 2 Tm 2:4]? By no means! For one wishing to live wickedly, the desert offers ample opportunity; the woods afford cover, and solitude assures silence. The evil that no one sees, no one censures.... In a convent, if you would do good, no one forbids it; if you wish to do evil, it is not permitted.... When others are present, you set them an example by your good life and give offence by a bad one.[70]

This is not so much a criticism of the eremetical life as a concern for the proper life for an individual person, with her own special spiritual state and in her own particular circumstances: "The wolf lurks in the wood. If you, a lamb, enter the dark of the wood, you offer prey to the wolf.... If you leave, you put yourself in danger, as I have tried to show. You will leave your sisters a legacy of scandal, and you will set the tongues of many wagging against you."[71]

Bernard's concern for the needs of the individual is also shown in his sensitive response to the departure of his nephew Robert from

Clairvaux for Cluny. Bernard blames himself for his earlier insensitivity to Robert's needs: "It was surely my fault that you left. I was too hard on a delicate young man, and I treated a tender youth with inhuman severity. This, as I remember, is why you then grumbled against me in my presence. And, in my absence, so I have heard, you do not cease to derogate me. I do not blame you for this."[72] Bernard does support the decision of some to change their way of life; others he discourages or turns away when they apply to Clairvaux. But always his counsel or decision is based on the good of the individual, not the abstract demands of a "higher" or "lower" life. And this is what justifies, for him, the variety of religious orders in the Church: "If any person, having chosen whatever order, rejects those living another life—or if that person suspects others spurn him or her—how could you rest securely in whatever vocation you have chosen? It is impossible for all the orders to hold [just] one person; it is impossible for all persons to hold to one order.... There is not just one path to follow, just as not only one [heavenly] room toward which we journey."[73] Cistercians who "derogate other orders" Bernard calls "citizens of Babylon, ... sons of darkness and children of Gehenna...."[74]

Despite Bernard's satirical description of Cluny's failings in his *Apology*, in that same work he declares: "This [Cluny's] way of life is holy and honorable. Chastity is its adornment; it is distinguished for its discretion. Instituted by the fathers, preordained by the Holy Spirit [see Ac 10:41], it is eminently suited for the salvation of souls. How could I condemn or despise that which I so praise?"[75] And Bernard's praise is based on personal experience:

> I remember how, on several occasions, I was received hospitably in monasteries of this order. May the Lord reward his servants [see 1 Sm 24:20] for the kindness—far more than what was necessary—which they showed me in my illness and for the honor they saw fit to give me—honor far greater than I deserved! I have asked them for their prayers. I have been present at their community meetings. I have often spoken with many of them about the Scriptures and the salvation of souls, both publicly in chapter and privately in parlors.[76]

Bernard translates his experience of Cluniac holiness into practice by discouraging the transfer to Cistercian cloisters of many Cluniac monks, including abbots, turning away those who come knocking, and returning to their own communities those who try to enter Clairvaux.[77]

This is why Bernard is so vehement in condemning what he regards as the pharisaical stance of some Cistercians in criticizing Cluny: "Clad in rough tunics we shrink from those clad in furs, as if it were not better to take possession of humility than to seize pride in tunics."[78] For Cistercians "to derogate the most glorious order of Cluny, to disparage impudently the holy men who so praiseworthily live within it, to insult the lights of the world from the darkness of our obscurity, is more than intolerable. In doing so we act, not like ravenous wolves in sheep's clothing [see Mt 7:15], but like biting fleas and gnawing worms [see Mt 6:19]...."[79] And Bernard takes this stand out of a firm conviction that a rigorous life is no guarantee of virtue:

> If, I say, we are pharisees who disdain others [see Lk 18:11] and, what is still more prideful, despise those better than ourselves, what advantage will we derive [see Gn 37:26; Jb 21:15] from our sparing and unappealing diet or from the well-known cheapness and roughness of our clothing? The heavy sweat of our daily labor, our binding discipline of fasting and vigils, all the unique and more austere practices of our life [see 2 Cor 11:27–28], will do us no good—unless we do all our works only so that we may be seen by others [see Mt 6:5].[80]

Virtue, not status, is the criterion of success in the monastic life—as it is in all others.

It is on this basis that Bernard can describe the Benedictine house of Saint Denis, newly reformed by its abbot, Suger, as "occupying virtue's highest height," as having "attained the most sublime pinnacle of merit."[81] Then, too, Bernard writes his treatise *On Precept and Dispensation* to answer Benedictine monks who have asked about their observance: "How can I, with good conscience, live a life not fully in accord with the *Rule* I have professed? Thus vowing but not delivering, am I not a perjurer?"[82] Bernard answers:

> It is perfectly legitimate that God be served in diverse ways in diverse monasteries. As long as one carefully observes the good customs of one's house, one is, without a doubt, living according to the *Rule,* for such good customs do not contradict the *Rule.* When one holds to the good which one finds being held in the place one has professed, one is truly living as one has promised. For this was doubtless that person's intention when pronouncing the vows, having seen the virtuous life of those living there when first determining and choosing to live with them.[83]

Bernard then turns from psychological and spiritual concerns to the institutional expression of those concerns:

> Must the monks of the great monastery [of Tours] follow the customs of Cluny, or the monks of Cluny follow the observances of Tours? Should, perhaps, both profess the strict, literal interpretation of the Cistercians? We all have made our vows according to the *Rule*—and in the very same words. But, since our implicit intention is not the same for all, we may, without a doubt, celebrate our different observances without endangering our salvation or condemning our profession. All—all good Christians, indeed—do not keep everything in the Gospel, yet they all live according to the Gospel....[84]

Be they Cistercians, Cluniacs, or other Benedictines,[85] all monks who follow the *Rule* faithfully are pleasing to God—and to Bernard.

But it is not only to other monks that Bernard offers his approval and friendship. Canons regular, including the Premonstratensians and Victorines,[86] the Gilbertines,[87] and also hermits,[88] as well as the semi-eremetical Carthusians,[89] receive help or encouragement or both from Bernard. Their ways of life are different from the Cistercian, but they are all valid. In them one can pursue virtue, and, in the end, this is what matters to Bernard.

C. CLERICAL "SUPERIORITY"

If some of Bernard's statements seem to make monasticism the "highest" calling, there are a number of passages in his works that seem to claim superiority for a life of preaching, a function he assigns especially to the clergy. Bernard writes, for example: "Rachel may be more beautiful, but Lia is more fertile [see Gn 29:17–31]. Let no one crave too much the kiss of contemplation, for better are the breasts of preaching."[90] Preaching, Bernard claims in one passage, is a more "manly" work than the contemplative prayer to which he has been called. And he has heard some people saying of him:

> "Why this waste [Mt 26:8]?" The reason was plainly that I lived for myself alone when, so they thought, I could be of use to many.... But let them who accuse me of indolence hear the Lord excusing me and replying for me: "Why do you trouble this woman [Mt 26:10]?" ... This is not a man, as you think, who can put his hand to strong things, but a woman [see Prv 31:19]. Why do you try to impose a burden on him that, to my mind, he cannot bear [see Ac 15:10]? The work he does for me is good [see Mk 14:6]. Let him remain in the good unless he gains the strength to do better. If he should progress from being a woman to manhood, to perfect manhood [see Eph 4:13], then he could take on the work of perfection."[91]

The work of perfection of which Bernard here speaks is the work of clerics, not monks:

> Brothers, let us honor bishops but stand in awe at their labors. If we were to think of their labors, we should not strive after their honors. Let us acknowledge our powers are unequal to their task; let us not be seduced into supposing that our soft, womanly shoulders could support the burdens of men. We should not scrutinize but honor them. You surely uncivilly censure their works whose burdens you escape. The woman

who sits at home spinning scolds inconsiderately her man returning from battle.[92]

And the "superior" task undertaken by clerics justifies behavior less circumspect than that demanded of monks.[93]

Bernard does not intend to assert the superiority of one way of life over another, but wishes to develop an appreciation for clerical life in monks who have chosen another way.[94] Bernard's rhetoric serves a twofold purpose: he wishes to impart to his fellow monks some of his understanding of the burdens of the clergy living in the world; he hopes, too, to dissuade them from ambition for honor in that world. Hyperbole does not automatically bring inconsistency.[95]

It is surely rhetorical humility that leads Bernard to place himself beneath a host of bishops both in "worth and office."[96] He is, in this case, writing to bishops whom he wishes to persuade to oppose one of their own number, and he adjusts his rhetoric to his audience. One must take such rhetoric seriously, of course. But one must also recognize rhetoric for what it is and not construct a theology from it—surely not a theology that would claim the innate superiority of the clerical office and vocation.

There is no doubt, however, that Bernard considers the life of the clergy in the world as indispensable to that world, and recognizes that the cleric's life brings with it grave dangers.[97] He writes the newly elected Pope Eugenius: "You have been called to a higher place, but not to a safer one."[98] Life in the world and service to the world bring the temptation to worldliness, to the adoption of "worldly" values.[99] As a corrective example, Bernard praises the poverty of some who minister to the needs of the world: "There are...men of good will [see Lk 2:14] who, desiring a truly Christian life, have exchanged riches for poverty and have set a small value on having or not having possessions. They have left all things behind them [see Mt 19:27] for the sake of him who left all things behind him for their sake, and they follow him wherever he goes [see Rv 14:4]."[100] The poverty Bernard extols is not so much a matter of choosing not to possess things but an attitude toward them. And this poverty is not only possible, but has been attained by virtuous clergy.

God calls some to one life, some to another,[101] but those who have heard a call to the clerical life must remain true to it. Bernard writes to Oger, a canon regular who resigned his pastoral office: "Either you ought not to have undertaken the rule of your flock or, having undertaken it, you should not have relinquished it.... For you have preferred your own counsel to that of God, choosing quiet for yourself rather than to devote yourself to the work which you have undertaken."[102]

Even monks must heed God's call to the care of souls in the clerical life, should the need arise. Bernard writes to Bernardo Pagenelli, his former novice at Clairvaux, newly chosen as bishop of Rome: "You chose to be the least in the house of your God and to take the lowest place at his banquet, but it has pleased him to say to the one whom he invited: 'Friend, go up higher [Lk 14:10].'"[103] But Bernard's "higher" means not that the life of the cleric is intrinsically superior, but merely that the monk chosen is "called by the Church to another office and another dignity."[104]

The Church's needs are not the only ones to be taken into account. The abilities of the individual monk must also be recognized. Despite Bernard's later acceptance of Bernardo's election to the bishopric of Rome, his first reaction was dismay at his fellow Cistercian's incapacity for the role.[105] Likewise, in refusing the archbishopric of Reims, Bernard appeals to his own inability to function in that office.[106] But, as always, it is the spiritual needs of the individual that are paramount in Bernard's mind. He writes to Pope Eugenius of the elevation of Hugh, abbot of Trois-Fontaines, to the cardinalate:

> The abbot of Trois-Fontaines was well planted because planted "by running waters [Ps 1:3]." But I fear that the good tree bearing good fruit [see Mt 7:17] will bear none if rooted out. We sometimes see a vine fruitful in its first planting, but sterile in its second. We see a well-planted tree flourish, only to wither when transplanted. You will gravely wound my heart [see Sg 4:9] if you do not send him back, for we are of "one heart and one soul [Ac 4:32]." As long as we are separated from one another, each part must be stained with its own blood.[107]

The needs of the individual person are essential in the choice of a ministry in the Church. It is not simply the perceived needs of the Church or the ability to meet that need that should drive the choice of a vocation. It is surely not the intrinsic superiority of one or another office in the Church.

D. The "Lowly" Laity

If Bernard believes that one's virtue depends not on one's vocation but on one's response to that calling, what is one to make of the occasional text that seems to denigrate the life of the laity? One such text occurs in Bernard's *First Sermon on the Nativity:* "...Let Job especially seek the fountain of wisdom, for he, more than the others [Noah and Daniel], walks in the midst of snares, so that it would seem a great thing indeed if he should avoid evil [see Ps 36:27]."[108] Lay folk, symbolized by Job, would seem from this to occupy a precarious place in Bernard's society and Church. Their place and path would seem merely lawful, though not expedient, in the quest for the happiness of salvation.[109] And yet Bernard also speaks of the laity's potential for virtue in terms of their proper motivation and not in terms of the relative value of their state of life or activities. He does so in his *Praise of the New Knighthood,* for example: "Danger or victory for a Christian [knight] depends on the disposition of his heart, not on the fortunes of war. If the reason for his fighting is good, the result of his fight cannot be evil, just as the results cannot be considered good when the reason is not good and the intention perverse."[110] How is one to account for this apparent discrepancy, this seeming inconsistency?

There seems no doubt that Bernard considers lay life both difficult and dangerous. Writing for his fellow Cistercian abbots, Bernard is emphatic on this:

> About the third group [symbolized by Job], the order of married layfolk, I shall touch only briefly, as such a consideration is less applicable to us. This third group surely consists of those who cross the wide sea [of life] by a ford both difficult

and dangerous. Their way is long, for they take no shortcuts. That their way is dangerous is clear in that, sad to say, so many are lost in it, while we see so few crossing it, as is necessary. Their way is very difficult, especially these days, when evil abounds, turning them from the straight path by the waves of this world, the whirlpools of vice, and the pitfalls of sin.[111]

But monks, too, face serious dangers, which Bernard enumerates in this same sermon.[112] Clerics also are subject to danger in their vocation.[113] In both cases, the most serious danger is the most fundamental of all vices: pride.

But dangers do not render any lifestyle unacceptable; indeed, all callings are quite able to produce heroic virtue.[114] The failings of all are washed clean in the fountain of God's mercy.[115] God's forgiveness is not necessary for much behavior of lay folk, while the same behavior is accounted sinful in clerics and monks. For Bernard, this goes beyond the obvious: it is not only that sex is legitimate for lay folk but not for clerics,[116] it is also true, for him, that "among lay folk frivolity is just frivolity—in the mouth of a priest it is blasphemy."[117]

But Bernard does not merely allow lay folk activities illicit for other social groups, he sees the laity as potential models for clerics and monks. Bernard's praise for Suger's reform of his abbey of Saint Denis likens Suger's virtues to those of a warrior: "In this [reform] you have acted like a knight bold in battle—or, rather, as a strong commander of a knightly host. When he sees his forces in flight and slaughtered on all sides by the swords of the enemy, though he sees he can save himself, he cheerfully chooses to die with them rather than bear the shame of living without them. So he stands fast in the battle; he fights stoutly."[118] In this letter to Suger, Bernard betrays both a surprising knowledge of military behavior and an ample appreciation for the virtues of lay folk who engage in battle.

But, Bernard believes, monks and clerics are to imitate the heroic virtue of lay folk, not their function. This is most obvious in Bernard's proscription of monastic involvement in the crusade.[119] The issue here is not that the life of the crusader is inherently inferior, for Bernard is capable of blocking a Knight Templar from becoming a monk.[120]

Clerics, too, are not to confuse their ministry with that of the laity. Bernard writes Suger of Saint Denis:

> Who would not be indignant; who would not murmur with secret tongue, that a deacon, contrary to the Gospel [see Mt 6:24], should serve equally God and mammon? That he, so elevated with ecclesiastical honors as to seem hardly inferior to bishops, should be so involved in military affairs that he should be set above commanders? I ask you, what sort of monster is this, who wishes to be seen simultaneously as both cleric and knight, but is neither one nor the other? But this is surely an abuse of both, that a deacon should be considered a minister of the king's table and that the king's seneschal should attend to the mysteries of the altar.... Is it more noble to be called a seneschal than a dean—than an archdeacon? It is indeed—but for a lay man, not a cleric, for a knight, not a deacon.... He completely confuses the states of life. He negligently abuses both offices by delighting in the pomp, not the military service of the world, delighting in the profit, not the cultivation of religion.[121]

Bernard insists that "clergy are not to fight with the arms of soldiers...,"[122] and even popes are not to dispense justice in secular affairs. Bernard writes Eugenius: "Your power is over sin, not over property, since it is because of sin, not property, that you have received the keys of the kingdom of heaven [see Mt 16:19], to exclude prevaricators, not possessors.... Why do you invade someone else's territory? Why do you put your sickle to someone else's harvest?"[123] Lay folk have their own function and dignity, which monks and clerics are not to usurp.[124]

Lay folk can change their station in life, Bernard thinks, if their motivation is mature and sincere, so that the change will promote their spiritual well-being. Bernard sends a young man to Clairvaux with a letter to Galcher, the prior:

> The youth who bears this letter to you I found awaiting me at Châlons. When he saw me, he asked me simply and

timidly to receive him into our order and make him a monk. He told me that, when Thomas of Marla, whose squire he had been, wished to make him a knight in service to the world, he preferred the service of Christ. For this reason he had recourse to us. Take counsel with some of the brethren about him, and, if they approve and you see fit, receive him and test his calling.[125]

Bernard approves not only transfers from lay to monastic life, but also shifts from lay to other sorts of vocations. He writes to Hugh, count of Champagne, who has become a Templar: "If it is for God's sake that you have created a common soldier out of a knight, a pauper out of a rich man, of this your growth I congratulate you—as is only right."[126] But, of course, Bernard's approval of a change from the lay life—occasional as it is, as hedged about with concern for proper motivation and the well-being of the individual concerned— does not imply a denigration of that lay life.

Indeed, in speaking to his monks in his *Twelfth Sermon on the Song of Songs,* Bernard presents a catalogue of the virtues of those living in the world:

> I have heard of . . . a rich man [Job] . . . who said: "No stranger ever had to stay outside; my door was open to travelers [Jb 31:32]." He also said: "I was the eye of the blind and the foot of the lame. I was the father of the poor. I broke the jaws of the wicked and snatched his prey from his teeth. Have I ever denied the poor what they wished or made the widow's eyes wait? Have I eaten my morsel alone, and the orphan not eaten of it? Have I ever despised one perishing without clothing and the poor person without covering? Has his heart not blessed me as he was warmed with the fleece of my sheep [see Jb 29:15–17; 31:16–17, 19–20]?" With what sweet smell this man must have besprinkled the earth! Each of his works bore its own aroma.[127]

Hospitality to the stranger, helpfulness to the afflicted, generous support of the poor, gentleness toward the contentious, and humility in service are not only virtues of lay folk long gone, but, Bernard counsels, ought to be the standards of lay behavior in all times.

It might be objected that Bernard addresses this sermon to monks, to encourage them in these virtues. But that is precisely the point. The virtues of all his social groups—monks, clerics, and lay folk—are, in the end, the same. Monks, clerics, and lay folk are all on the path of perfection, all cross the sea of life with prospect of success. Thus, lay folk can cheerfully be used as models for monks.

IX
Resolving Some Apparent Inconsistencies

A. The Chimaera of His Age

If Bernard distinguishes clearly the spheres of action of the monk and cleric, how is one to explain his own extensive activity in the world?[1] It surely comes as no surprise that Bernard did not spend all his monastic life at Clairvaux. Both Robert Fossier[2] and Jean Leclercq[3] have estimated that Bernard spent at least one-third of his abbatiate away from his monastery—and those, I suspect, are conservative estimates. Some of Bernard's absences were surely on the business of his order, but—again it comes as no surprise—much of his travel was not properly monastic by his own definition. Many of his contemporaries must have thought of him as Bernard *from* Clairvaux rather than *of* Clairvaux. Despite Bernard's injunctions to others to flee the world,[4] he spent much of his time in the world or for the world, ordering the affairs of Church and state and confronting contemporary problems—all this by means of letters, treatises, preaching, and other forms of activity that he himself declared were not the business of the monk but of the cleric. How are we to understand his action in settling the papal schism of 1120,[5] in preaching a crusade,[6] in attempting to put down rebellion[7] and prevent warfare?[8] These are, after all, activities[9] he assigned to bishops and other clergy and to lay rulers.[10]

Some of the activities that called Bernard from his cloister were so manifestly not the concern of a monk that Bernard's involvement drew criticism from members of the Roman curia. Bernard details this criticism and answers it in a letter to Cardinal Haimeric, the papal chancellor, and his colleagues:

> What have I done to displease your brotherhood, good men? Is it because, at Châlons, a man discredited on all sides was removed from his stewardship [see Mt 24:51] for squandering the goods of his lord in the church of Verdun over which he had been placed? Or because, at Cambrai, Fulbert, who was clearly ruining his monastery, was forced to cede his post to Parvin, who is, by all accounts, a faithful and prudent servant [see Mt 24:45]? Or, perhaps, because, at Laon, the Lord's sanctuary was returned to him after having been a brothel of Venus?[11]

Bernard acknowledges that his presence on these occasions is irregular, but he excuses himself by appealing to the necessity of obedience:

> It is my whole and only fault that I was present on these occasions, I who am only fit to live hidden away, I who am my own judge, accuser, and witness to what extent my actions correspond to my profession and the name of monk which I bear is translated into a solitary life. I was present; I do not deny it. But I was summoned there; I was dragged there. If this displeases our friends, I confess it displeases me as well. Would I had not gone to those councils; would I should never need to go on like occasions![12]

Bernard is painfully aware of the inconsistency of his activity in the world with his profession as a monk.

The Second Crusade provides an excellent illustration of the conflict between Bernard's view of his vocation and his action in the world. It is clear that Bernard thinks the crusading endeavor, however worthy it may be in itself,[13] is not the business of monks. Cistercians cannot be crusaders, he writes to his fellow monks—monks entreating their abbots for permission to join the crusading host: "Why do you [wish to] appear clothed in the crusader's cross, you who do not cease to bear the cross in your hearts—if you follow your [own] way in religion? To be brief, I say (by apostolic authority, not my own): if a monk or *conversus* goes on this expedition, he will place himself under the binding sentence of excommunication."[14] Bernard was equally vehement in denouncing the earlier effort of his fellow Cistercian abbot, Arnold of Morimund, who had resolved to set out on a pilgrimage to Jerusalem. On that occasion, Bernard had written Pope Callixtus II:

> ...One of my brother abbots, the abbot of Morimund, has ill-advisedly deserted the monastery over which he has been set and, impelled by a fickle spirit, has resolved to rush off to Jerusalem. But first, they say, he will test your watchful prudence by trying, in any way he can, to extort permission for his error from you. If you were to give your assent—which God forbid—consider how much harm this could cause to our order. With such an example, any abbot who felt burdened by the weight of his pastoral care would soon cast it aside—perceiving it permissible to cast it off—especially among us [Cistercians] where there are grave burdens to carry and little honor in carrying them....If he says, as I have been told, that he wishes to plant the observances of our order in that land, and this is why he takes with him a flock of the brothers, who could not see that what is wanted there is fighting soldiers and not singing and praying monks?[15]

Bernard does encourage Premonstratensians to undertake the journey to Jerusalem and plant their houses there,[16] but Premonstratensians are regular canons, not monks; they are clerics whose work is properly in the world.

Bernard was a reluctant participant in crusading ventures. To Pope Eugenius he voiced his reluctance when chosen leader of a planned expedition to repair the catastrophic results of the Second Crusade:

> Unless I am mistaken, you have by now heard how the Council of Chartres—I wonder by what judgment—chose

me as leader and chief of the army. You may be quite certain it neither was nor is with my counsel or agreement, and that it is beyond my powers, as I gauge them, to do such a thing. Who am I to arrange the siege of castles, to march out in front of armed soldiers? And what could be more remote from my calling—even supposing I had the power, even if I were not lacking the skill?[17]

Bernard is well aware of the dilemma, but this does not explain his having preached the crusade that had failed.

Bernard's role in settling the double election of Innocent II and Anacletus II in 1130 presents another apparent inconsistency. If we are to believe Bernard's Benedictine biographer, Arnold of Bonneval, the decision for Innocent was Bernard's. At the Council of Étampes, called to decide the matter for France,

when the bishops and nobles assembled in the council for which they had prepared by fasting and prayer, they unanimously decided that the work of God—the judgment on the competitors' claims—should be left to the servant of God. Bernard diligently examined the order and procedure of the two elections and the merits, lives, and reputations of the two candidates. Filled with the Holy Spirit and speaking in the name of all, he declared Innocent the legitimate pontiff. This decision the whole assembly approved.[18]

Whether or not this is exactly the way the decision was made,[19] there is no doubt Bernard would engage in a vigorous campaign of letter writing and travel on behalf of his choice.[20] Bernard opens this campaign with a vehement defense of Innocent's claim:

Those who are God's unite themselves freely to him; those who stand against him are either the Antichrist's or the Antichrist himself.... Have not all the princes recognized [see Jn 7:26] that he is truly the elect of God [see Lk 23:35]? The kings of France, of England, of Spain, and, finally, of Rome have received Innocent as pope and have each recognized him as the bishop of their souls [see 1 Pt 2:25] .... The choice of the better part of the cardinals, the approval of the majority of the people, and—what is more powerful than these—the witness of his good life commend Innocent to all and establish him as the supreme pontiff.[21]

But Bernard's vehemence does not explain his involvement in the schism or in any other of the affairs of the world.

Bernard is also vehement in rejecting that involvement: "Have I ever asked from my lord [the pope; see 2 K 4:28] that churches be set in order by me, that I dispose of bishoprics, that I create bishops? I am as apt an instrument for these things as an ant in pulling a cart."[22] These activities are the proper function of the clergy, as is the ministry of preaching. Bernard writes to Archbishop Henry of Mainz about the renegade monk, Radulf: "If he boasts of being a monk or hermit, and on that basis assumes for himself the liberty or office of preaching, he can and should know that a monk does not have the office of teaching but of lamenting. A monk should be one for whom a town is a prison and solitude a paradise."[23] Prayer is the role of the monk in the Church, as Bernard writes to his sons at Clairvaux: "'Pray for the things which promote the peace [Ps 121:6]' of the Church. Pray for the things which promote our salvation. Pray that I may see you once more, live with you once more, die in your presence. And so live that you may obtain that for which you pray. ... Pray for the lord pope, who cherishes me and all of you with paternal affection. Pray for the lord chancellor, who is like a mother to me, and for all those who are with him ...."[24] Ironically, Bernard writes this letter while away from Clairvaux on non-monastic business of the Church.

Yet, Bernard insists, monks are not to leave their monasteries. In his seventh *Parable*, Bernard presents a dialogue between the Lord and a monk which ends:

LORD: "... But tell me, I pray, my businessman, where did you do business? Where have you made these profits? Where have you acquired these things?"

MONK: "In the monastery, in the cloister, in claustral discipline. This is the place of such business; this is the means by which such profits are possible. I do not recall having gained any profit from by going out from it."

LORD: "O happy are those whose house is a monastery! I make you an apostle to your brothers. Tell them for me not to delight in going out of their monastic enclosure frequently or for long, or in wandering abroad, for in their cloister they have such great riches and the means to such profit."[25]

Bernard knows there is only one place where his spiritual health is secure. He writes Pope Innocent II:

After long delay and many labors born in the service of the Roman church, it pleased you to allow my return to my brothers. My body was broken "like an evil doer [2 Tm 2:9]"; yet I arrived at my monastery in good condition, rejoicing with the sheaves [see Ps 125:6] of peace. I believed I had escaped labor for rest. I hoped I might be allowed to repair somewhat the damage to my spiritual life and the loss in holy quiet which I suffered while outside my monastery....[26]

The spiritual losses Bernard suffers in leaving his cloister are a source of no little anguish to him:

Happy are those hidden in the tabernacle of the Lord in evil times, trusting in the shadow of his wings "until iniquity passes away [Ps 56:2]"! As for me, I am an unhappy man, poor and naked, a man born for labor [see Jb 5:7]. I am a chick without feathers, almost always exiled from my little nest, exposed to wind and storm. Like a drunk I am confused and troubled, and all my senses have been consumed.[27]

It is not only Bernard's own spiritual hunger for the cloister that makes him regret his actions in the world. He is also concerned with the welfare of his monastic family, deprived of its father during his many absences. He writes his sons and brothers at Clairvaux:

> On the basis of your own experience, consider what I suffer. If you have been troubled by my absence, let no one doubt it has been more troublesome to me. We are not equally dejected; we do not have equal reason for complaint. You are deprived of one; I am deprived of all of you. I am filled with care for just as many folk as there are monks at Clairvaux. ...Not only do I grieve that I am driven to live for a time without you—without whom to be king would seem to me a sorry servitude—but I am also compelled to engage in matters which disturb all feelings of quiet and which are, perhaps, incompatible with my vocation.[28]

The burden of Bernard's absence from his monks and his fear that in this way he has left them spiritually undernourished drives Bernard to write another letter to his monks: "This is the third time, unless I am mistaken, that those whom I hold in my heart have been torn away from me. My infants have been weaned before their time; those I have begotten by the Gospel [see 1 Cor 4:15] I am not allowed to rear. I am obliged to desert my own and to care for others. I do not know which is more cruelly painful, to be taken away from the former or to be entangled in the latter."[29] On one occasion, in responding to Innocent's call for Bernard's presence at the papal curia, he excuses himself in this way: "I do not say: 'I have bought five yoke of oxen' or 'I have married a wife [Lk 14:19–20].' But clearly, as you well know, I must nurse my infants [see 1 Cor 3:1–2], and I do not see how I can come without being a serious obstacle and danger to them."[30] Given that it is not the monk's vocation to engage in the affairs of the world in however worthy a cause, given that Bernard sees a threat in such activity to his own spiritual welfare and that of his sons at Clairvaux, why does Bernard involve himself in the affairs of the world, in affairs pertaining to the vocation of the clergy living in and responsible for the well-being of the world?

Many times Bernard's actions in the world are reluctant responses to earnest entreaties to do so.[31] But some do not merely beg Bernard's involvement; many persons of great authority command his involvement in non-monastic matters. Bernard's role in the Italian phase of the papal schism, for example, was a response to "the urgent request of the emperor, the apostolic command, and the prayers of princes and the Church...."[32] Bernard sometimes complains at the need for this obedience, especially in matters which he considers beyond his competence and ability. He writes Cardinal Haimeric: "...Does it please you that I am burdened with these matters and occupied with such business?...I consider nothing safer for me than to obey the pope's wishes, but I wish he would pay attention to what is possible for me. Truly, I wish he would learn that such things I cannot do—or how difficult it is for me to do them!"[33] However, Bernard will reluctantly respond to the call of legitimate authority demanding his involvement in the affairs of the world:

> ...I know it has been my plan and purpose never to leave my monastery except on the business of my order—unless called by the legate of the apostolic see or, certainly, by my own bishop. As you well know, a person of my humble state must obey any order of these authorities, except by the privilege of some higher authority. If ever, as I hope, my hands could receive this [privilege] through your hands, then without a doubt I shall have peace and peace would go out from me. But, even if I am hidden away and silent, I do not think the murmuring of the churches will cease—if the Roman curia does not stop doing the will of those in attendance [there], to the prejudice of those absent.[34]

Here a new motive is added. Bernard's reluctant obedience to the authority of those commanding his activity is matched by his irritation at the injustice of some contemporary ecclesiastical practices.

Indeed, Bernard often appeals to the crying need of the Church to justify his involvement in the world. He writes Pope Honorius II: "The tears of the bishops, the complaint of the whole Church, we, however unworthy, who are also her sons, can in no way ignore. Of that which we see, we must speak. A great need draws us from the cloister into the public arena...."[35] For example, the "crying needs" of the church of Tours lead Bernard to respond to Pope Innocent's commission to heal the schism there.[36] Bernard's concern for the needs of the Church at home is matched by his care for the needs of the Church in the Holy Land. These needs justify, in his eyes, the involvement of monks, his own and those of Peter the Venerable, abbot of Cluny, to whom he writes:

> The Son of God turns to you as one of the great rulers of his household [see Ps 104:21].... It is necessary that, in his need, he discern your aid and counsel. Little or nothing concerning God's enterprise was achieved by us at the meeting at Chartres. Your presence there was much desired and awaited. Another meeting, at Compiègne, has been announced for the ides of July. We beg, we implore you to be there. It is necessary for you to be there; necessity, great necessity, demands it.[37]

When it is necessity that calls Bernard from his cloister, he is confident that God will supply him and his orphaned monks with the spiritual sustenance to overcome the difficulties of his absence.[38]

In the same letter in which Bernard assures his monks of this, he adds another reason for his involvement in the affairs of the world. He tells them: "I serve willingly, for love gives me freedom. To this willing service I challenge you, you who are dear to my heart. Serve in this love which casts out fear [see 1 Jn 4:18], which notices no labor, which is oblivious to merit, which needs no reward, which, nevertheless, impels as nothing else can."[39] It is not only that love covers a multitude of Bernard's absences from his monastery, he will even take the initiative in outside affairs in response to the prompting of love. He writes Pope Honorius: "... I do not fear to address you, especially on a matter which love prompts. I speak, my lord, of the Church of Châlons; for I will not, I may not—as far as in me lies—conceal the peril which threatens it."[40] Thus Bernard's actions in the world are prompted not only by need or in obedient response to command, but by love: "I dare [to write again, Honorius], prompted by Lady Love, who also commands you."[41] Love, then, justifies action—even action not proper to one's state of life—as long as that love is ordered by him who is Love himself.[42]

Bernard's action in the world does not contradict his social and ecclesiological principles—principles that separate the ways of life and spheres of activity of monk and cleric. Bernard's action is explicable in terms of this theory: obedience, grave necessity, and, above all, love may demand the monk's active response to the needs of the Church in the world. Still, Bernard's activity in that world is a great burden to him and evokes this cry:

> My monstrous life, my troubled conscience cries out to you. I am something like the chimaera of my age—neither cleric nor lay. For I have now cast off the life of the monk, though not the habit. I do not wish to write to you of what I suppose you have heard from others about me: what I have been doing, what I am trying to do, through what dangers I am driven in the world or, rather, down what precipices I am hurled.[43]

Bernard is indeed the chimaera of his age, but, whether viewed as a lion, dragon, or goat, the monster from Clairvaux knows what he is doing.

B. A Concluding Illustration: Art and Society

A concrete example of Bernard's appreciation of all social classes, of his sensitivity to the needs of all states of life, is his teaching on art.[44] To be sure, Bernard's response to Cluniac monastic buildings in his *Apology to Abbot William* seems a crushing condemnation of architectural beauty. "I shall say nothing," he writes, "of the soaring heights, the extravagant lengths, and the unnecessary widths of the churches. I shall say nothing of the lavish decorations and the curious images, the sight of which ensnares those who are there to pray and impedes their good disposition...."[45] But Bernard does not say nothing; he says a great deal.

He questions not only the sumptuous dimensions and decorations of Cluniac architecture but also the motivation for this grandeur: "Of this I ask, as a monk to monks, what an ancient writer [Perseus] asked of his fellow ancients: 'Tell me, O priests, what is this gold doing in the holy place?' I, however—more concerned with the sense than the text—say: 'Tell me, O poor men—if you truly are poor men—what is this place?'"[46] Bernard proceeds to answer his own question in scathing terms:

> To speak plainly, is not avarice, which is the service of idols [see Eph 5:5; Col 3:5], the reason for all this [elaborate decoration]? With it do we not seek gifts rather than fruitful enjoyment? If you ask: "how?," I shall answer: "By a truly marvelous means." There is a way of spreading money abroad so that it multiplies. It is spent so that it may increase, and profusion gives birth to abundance. By this sumptuous appearance, which is really a wondrous deception, people are roused more to giving than to prayer. Thus riches are drunk up by riches; thus wealth carries off wealth. By some means which I do not understand, where more riches are seen, there offerings pour in more freely.[47]

But of course Bernard understands very well how monks use wealth to gain more wealth:

> Eyes observe golden reliquaries, and coffers are opened. Display a beautiful picture of any saint, and the saint is believed holier if the picture is more brilliantly embellished. People rush to kiss the picture, and they are invited to donate. The beauty is more admired than the holiness venerated. This is the reason churches are decked out with bejeweled crowns ... radiant with ornamental stones. Instead of candle-sticks we see tree-like structures, heavy with much metal and of exquisite fabrication, glittering no more from the candles than from their jewels. What do you think is the reason for all this? The compunction of penitents—or the admiration of

onlookers? O vanity of vanities [see Qo 1:2], but not more vain than insane.[48]

Avarice, not aesthetics, is the issue at stake, for all this grandeur is purchased at the expense of the poor: "The walls of the church glitter, but within it the poor go needy. Gold covers its stones, and its children are left naked. The eyes of the rich are served at the expense of the needy. Ways are found to delight the curious, but not to sustain the unfortunate."[49] Bernard's concerns are not aesthetic but moral, it would seem, and his conclusion seems to be that beauty is to be rejected in favor of charity.

But this picture is incomplete. Indeed, it seems totally contradicted by Bernard's letter to the people of Rome chiding them for despoiling the beauty of their churches:

> Ponder the reason, think on the end, consider by whom and for whose benefit the adornments and wealth of all the churches in your city have so recently been squandered. Whatever gold and silver could be found on the altars, in the vessels of the altar, on the sacred images themselves, has been pillaged and carried off by impious hands. What of all this do you now find in your purses? Its former beauty has been irretrievably lost to the Lord's house.[50]

Here there is not only a moral question—the cupidity of the looters, which Bernard does indeed condemn—but also an aesthetic question —the beauty, which Bernard praises, of the churches looted. How is one to reconcile this with Bernard's apparent condemnation of beauty in the *Apology*?

The answer lies in the artistic distinctions Bernard makes in that same treatise: "The situation is different for bishops than for monks. We know that bishops are obligated to both the wise and the foolish [see Rom 1:14]. By use of material ornamentation, they arouse the devotion of their people, whose involvement in material matters makes them less open to the spiritual. We monks, however, have gone forth from the folk and have abandoned for Christ all that is precious and splendid to the world . . . ."[51] Thus, the artistic ornamentation that constitutes an incitement to devotion for lay folk becomes a distraction in the monastic life. This is why Bernard is free with his satire when criticizing highly decorated monastic architecture:

> In the cloisters, where the brothers are supposed to do their meditative reading, what excuse is there for these ridiculous monstrosities, this wondrously deformed beauty and beautiful deformity? Why there these dirty apes? Why these wild lions? Why these monstrous centaurs? Why these figures half man and half beast? Why these striped tigers? Why these battling knights? Why these trumpeting hunters? You see one head with many bodies and one body with many heads. Here we see a quadruped with the tail of a serpent, there a fish with the head of a quadruped. There a beast that is horse in front and goat behind; here an animal with horns and the rear of a horse. Everywhere appears such a great and amazing variety of diverse forms that one might rather prefer to read from the marble walls than from books. One could spend one's whole day marveling at one of these, rather than in meditating on the law of the Lord [see Ps 1:2]. Good God! Even if one is not ashamed of the absurdities, why is one not annoyed at the expense?[52]

Such architectural decoration is inappropriate to the activity carried on within the building, and this is the reason Bernard rejects it. Monastic meditation requires concentration, and so distraction—even the distraction of beautiful or wondrous objects—is inappropriate to the life style of the monk.

But Bernard does not reject beauty—not even for monks. He describes the building of the restored monastery of Bangor by his friend Malachy of Armagh:

> . . . Behold! An oratory appeared, built of great stones and extremely beautiful. He paid great attention to its site, form, and composition. . . . So soundly and attentively did he note, so diligently did he observe everything concerning place,

manner, and quality, that, once the work was finished, the completed oratory appeared so like the one he had envisioned that he, like Moses, could hear it said: "See that you make everything according to the pattern which was shown you on the mountain [Heb 8:5]."[53]

Care should be taken to make monasteries beautiful, but that beauty should be appropriate to the function of the building.

Aesthetical questions aside, there is much to be learned of Bernard's view of Church and society from his views on art. What is appropriate for lay folk and the clerics who minister to them is not appropriate for monks. Money ill-spent on elaborate decoration by monks becomes money well-spent by clerics on churches, the decoration of which will inspire lay folk. Each social group has its own place and function; each has its own needs.

And all are necessary to a happily ordered society and a Church on her pilgrim path to perfection. Bernard writes in his *Forty-sixth Sermon on the Song of Songs:*

> "Our little bed is covered with flowers; the beams of our houses are of cedar, the paneling of cypress [Sg 1:15–16]." ...It should be noted how beautifully every state in the Church is comprehended in one brief expression: the authority of prelates, the moral dignity of the clergy, the virtuous behavior of the people, the peacefulness of the monks. Truly, when all is well [see 2 K 5:21] with these, holy mother Church rejoices in considering them. And then she offers them too to the gaze of her beloved [Bridegroom], since she refers all to his goodness as the author of all things—attributing nothing to herself.... She says "our little bed" and "the beams of our houses" and "our paneling," thus boldly associating herself in possession with him to whom she knows herself united in love.[54]

Lay folk, prelates, clerics, and monks make up the Church that is united to her divine Bridegroom.

This is the vision of Church and society of a Cistercian monk—a monk in whom the people of his time placed their confidence. And, we might note again, Bernard's life and vision embodied many values of his age, as is evidenced by its very choice of him as its leader.[55] Bernard saw himself as the tongue of the body that is the Church,[56] and that Church and society most often conceded him the role.

Notes

I. Bernard, Society, and the Church

1. See Arnold of Bonneval, *Sancti Bernardi abbatis Clarae-Vallensis vita et res gestae [Vita prima], Liber secundus* 1.3; PL 185:270.

2. See Elizabeth Kennan, "The 'De consideratione' of St. Bernard of Clairvaux and the Papacy in the Mid-Twelfth Century: A Review of Scholarship," *Traditio* 23 (1967) 92, n. 80.

3. See Ep 124 (SBOp 7:305–7; James 188–89), Ep 125 (SBOp 7:307–8; James 189–90), Ep 126 (SBOp 7:309–19; James 190–99), Ep 127 (SBOp 7:320–21), Ep 129 (SBOp 7:322–24; James 200–201), Ep 130 (SBOp 7:325–26; James 201–2), Ep 131 (SBOp 7:326–28; James 208–9), Ep 132 (SBOp 7:328–29; James 204), Ep 133 (SBOp 7:329; James 207), Ep 137 (SBOp 333; James 207), Ep 138 (SBOp 7:334; James 209), and Ep 139 (SBOp 7:335–36; James 210–11).

4. Martha G. Newman, *The Boundaries of Charity: Cistercian Culture and Ecclesiastical Reform, 1098–1180* (Stanford, California: Stanford University Press, 1996), p. 196.

5. See Jean Leclercq, "Saint Bernard on the Church," *The Downside Review* 85 (1967) 282–83. Paschal Phillips offers a cautionary note on the extent of Bernard's influence in "The Presence—and Absence—of Bernard of Clairvaux in the Twelfth-Century Chronicles," in *Bernardus Magister*, pp. 35–53. Giles Constable offers a balanced assessment in his *The Reformation of the Twelfth Century* (Cambridge: Cambridge University Press, 1996), pp. 108–9: "Bernard stands out as one of the few figures of his time (or, indeed, of any time) who was equally important as a writer and as a man of affairs. While he may have been somewhat less influential than some writers have suggested, since he by no means always got his way, it is clear that few contemporaries could resist his moral force and powers of persuasion."

6. See, for example, Virginia G. Berry, "The Second Crusade," in *A History of the Crusades* (ed. Kenneth M. Setton), I, *The First Hundred Years*

(ed. Marshall W. Baldwin) (Madison, Milwaukee, and London: The University of Wisconsin Press, 1969), pp. 463–512. For a more specifically bernardine account, see André Seguin, "Bernard et la seconde Croisade," in *Bernard de Clairvaux,* pp. 379–409.

7. Ep 247.2; SBOp 8:141; James 399.

8. See Odo of Deuil, *De profectione Ludovici VII in orientem* 1; ed. and trans. Virginia Gingerick Berry (New York: W. W. Norton & Company Inc., 1948), p. 8.

9. See the *Sancti Bernardi abbatis Clarae-Vallensis vita et res gestae, Liber sextus seu miracula a sancto Bernardo per Germaniam, Belgium Galliamque patrata, anno 1146* 4.15; PL 185:381–82.

10. See Otto of Freising, *Gesta Friderici I. imperatoris* 1.42; in G. Waitz and B. de Simpson (eds.), *Monumenta Germaniae historica, Scriptores rerum Germanicarum in usum scholarum...*, 46, 3rd ed. (Hannover, Leipzig: Impensis Bibliopolii Hahniani, 1912), pp. 60–61.

11. Watkin Williams gives the figure of 300,000 to 400,000 men, based on the numbers—probably exaggerated—he has found in contemporary sources. See Williams's *Saint Bernard of Clairvaux* (Manchester: Manchester University Press, 1935, reprinted 1953), pp. 281–82.

12. SBOp 7 and 8.

13. A good general survey of Bernard's contributions to theology may be found in *Saint Bernard théologien: Actes du Congrès de Dijon, 15–19 Septembre 1953,* ASOC 9 (1953) fasc. 3–4, 2nd ed. (Roma: Editiones Cistercienses, 1954), *passim.*

14. Jean Leclercq, *Bernard of Clairvaux and the Cistercian Spirit,* trans. Claire Lavoie, CS 16 (Kalamazoo, Michigan: Cistercian Publications, 1976), p. 96. See also John Eudes Bamberger, "The Influence of St Bernard," *CSQ* 25 (1990) 101–14, especially pp. 104–8.

15. Jean Leclercq, *Monks and Love in Twelfth-Century France: Psycho-Historical Essays* (Oxford: at the Clarendon Press, 1979), pp. 106–7.

16. See Leclercq, "Saint Bernard on the Church," p. 274.

17. SC 57.3; SBOp 2:120–21; CF 31:97–98. See III Sent 97; SBOp 6/2:155; CF 55:314.

18. SC 78.3; SBOp 2:268; CF 40:132.

19. SC 25.2; SBOp 1:164; CF 7:51.

20. Leclercq, "Saint Bernard on the Church," pp. 274–75. See SC 68.2; SBOp 2:197; CF 40:18–19.

21. Pent 3.8; SBOp 5:176; CF 53:87.

22. SC 80.1; SBOp 2:277; CF 40:146.

23. O Pasc 1.5; SBOp 5:115; Luddy 2:214.

24. SC 68.1; SBOp 2:196; CF 40:17.

25. SC 68.3; SBOp 2:198; CF 40:20.

26. See SC 68.4; SBOp 2:198; CF 40:20.

27. See Yves Congar, "Die Ekkesiologie des hl. Bernhard," in *Bernhard von Clairvaux,* p. 78.

28. Ep 78.9; SBOp 7:207; James 115.

29. SC 65.1; SBOp 2:172; CF 31:179.

30. Mich 1.5; SBOp 5:297; Luddy 3:321. See Thomas Renna, "The City in Early Cistercian Thought," *Cîteaux* 34 (1983) 5–19. Congar gives a list of references to the Church as the body of Christ in "Die Ekkesiologie," on p. 108, n. 32.

31. SC 76.8; SBOp 2:259; CF 40:116.

32. Ep 243.2; SBOp 8:131; James 391–92.

33. See *Spiritual Teachings,* p. 209. An earlier and much shorter version of some of the material in this section may be found in my "The Social Theory of Bernard of Clairvaux," in Joseph F. O'Callaghan (ed.), *Studies in Medieval Cistercian History Presented to Jeremiah F. O'Sullivan,* CS 13 (Spencer, Massachusetts: Cistercian Publications, 1971), pp. 35–40. A good survey of Bernard's teaching on various vocations is Raphael Fritegotto, *De vocatione christiana s. Bernardi doctrina,* Studia Antoniana 15 (Roma: Pontificum Athenaeum Antonianum, 1961).

34. Abb 1; SBOp 5:288; Luddy 3:306. Bernard Jacqueline points out that Gregory the Great, following Origen and Augustine, makes the same distinction. See "Saint Grégoire le Grand et l'ecclésiologie de saint Bernard," *Coll* 36 (1974) 72.

35. Abb 1; SBOp 5:289; Luddy 3:306–7.

36. Div 9.3; SBOp 6/1:119.

37. See Nat 1.7; SBOp 4:249; Luddy 1:388. The mercy of God extends even to those who have gravely sinned. See Ep 363.3; SBOp 8:313.

38. Div 40.9; SBOp 6/1:242; Luddy 3:458. See also Par 6 (SBOp 6/2:294; CF 55:82) and V Nat 3.9 (SBOp 4:218–19; Luddy 1:340–41).

39. JB 3; SBOp 5:178; CF 53:90.

40. Par 6; SBOp 6/2:286; CF 55:71.

41. SC 22.8; SBOp 1:134; CF 7:20.

42. SC 12.11; SBOp 1:67; CF 4:86.

43. SC 12.11; SBOp 1:67; CF 4:86.

44. SC 12.11; SBOp 1:67; CF 4:86.

45. SC 12.11; SBOp 1:67; CF 4:86.

46. SC 66.9; SBOp 2:183–84; CF 31:200.

47. Csi 5.5.12; SBOp 3:476; CF 37:154.

48. The *Apology* has generally been discussed with an eye to its criticism of the Cluniac way of life. See, for example, M. D. Knowles, *Cistercians & Cluniacs: The Controversy Between St. Bernard and Peter the Venerable,* Friends of Dr. Williams's Library, Ninth Lecture, 1955 (London, New York, Toronto: Geoffry Cumberlege; Oxford University Press, 1955), *passim*. Vincentius Hermans maintains, however, that the *Apology* was written to praise Cluny rather than to detract from its glory. See "De h. Bernardus en de stichters van Cîteaux," in *Sint Bernardus van Clairvaux,* p. 44. Jean Leclercq amplifies this: "...The *Apology* is not to be taken as an historical document that proposes to teach us about the Cluniac observances it denounces. It is a pamphlet destined to help its recipients by 'reproving' them. It requires therefore a certain measure of irony and exaggeration. Humor can surpass the limits of good taste— not the case here—but it is legitimate and one should not be misled by it." *Bernard of Clairvaux and the Cistercian Spirit,* p. 29.

49. Apo 3.5; SBOp 3:84–85; CF 138–39.

50. Apo 3.5; SBOp 3:85; CF 1:39.

51. See Apo 3.5; SBOp 3:85; CF 1:40.

52. Apo 3.6; SBOp 3:86; CF 1:40.

53. Apo 3.6–4.7; SBOp 3:86–87; CF 1:41.

54. Apo 4.8; SBOp 3:88; CF 1:43.

55. Apo 4.8; SBOp 3:88; CF 1:43–44.

56. SC 49.5; SBOp 2:76; CF 31:26.

57. Apo 4.9; SBOp 3:89; CF 1:44.

II. The Monastic Order of Daniel

1. This section has been immeasurably enriched by the work of Bede Lackner. See "The Monastic Life According to Saint Bernard," in John R. Sommerfeldt (ed.), *Studies in Medieval Cistercian History, II,* CS 24 (Kalamazoo, Michigan: Cistercian Publications, 1976), pp. 49–62. See also Hugh McCaffery, "The Basics of Monastic Living in St Bernard," *CSQ* 25 (1990) 157–62. An earlier version of this section may be found in my "The Monk and Monastic Life in the Thought of Bernard of Clairvaux," *Word and Spirit: A Monastic Review* 12 (1990) 43–53.

2. See above p. 6.

3. Abb 3; SBOp 5:290; Luddy 3:309.

4. Abb 3; SBOp 5:290–91; Luddy 3:309–10.

5. Ep 126.10; SBOp 7:317; James 197. Among the monks Bernard mentions are the Camaldolese, Vallambrosians, Carthusians, Cluniacs, and "the brethren of Caen, Tiron, and Savigny."

6. Div 22.1; SBOp 6/1:170; Luddy 3:541.

7. Mt 19:21; quoted in, for example, Div 27.3; SBOp 6/1:199.

8. Ep 64.1–2; SBOp 7:157–58; James 91.

9. Div 42.4; SBOp 6/1:258; Luddy 3:532.

10. Div 42.4; SBOp 6/1:258; Luddy 3:531. See III Sent 29 (SBOp 6/2:84; CF 55:216) and III Sent 91 (SBOp 6/2:140–41; CF 55:290–91).

11. Par 7; SBOp 6/2:302; CF 55:99.

12. Bernard also describes the monastery as a prison. See Ep 385.4 (SBOp 8:353; James 492) and Ep 227 (SBOp 8:97; James 373). Yet that prison is "an open jail without chains" (Ded 1.2; SBOp 5:371). "The fruit of [this] captivity" is the Father himself (QH 9.1; SBOp 4:435–36; CF 25:182).

13. Csi 4.4.11; SBOp 3:457; CF 37:123.

14. SC 46.2; SBOp 2:56; CF 7:241.

15. See Par 1.6; SBOp 6/2:265; CF 55:23–24.

16. Ep 322.1; SBOp 8:257; James 449. For Bernard's use of maternal imagery, see Caroline Walker Bynum, *Jesus as Mother: Studies in the Spirituality of the High Middle Ages* (Berkeley, Los Angeles, London: University of California Press, 1984), pp. 115–18.

17. Leclercq, *Bernard of Clairvaux and the Cistercian Spirit,* p. 37.

18. Ep 142.1; SBOp 7:340; James 220.

19. See *Spiritual Teachings,* pp. 80–87 and 119–203.

20. Ep 143.2; SBOp 7:343; James 212.

21. Ep 1.4; SBOp 7:4; James 4. Bernard's references to manual labor are most often literal reflections of that activity. Occasionally, however, working the land is an image of the effort needed to properly direct the will. See Par 7; SBOp 6/2:300; CF 55:95.

22. SC 9.2; SBOp 1:43; CF 4:54.

23. RB 58. The *Rule* begins with an admonition to "turn the ear of your heart..." (RB, prol.). Obedience is due not only to the abbot, but to all the brethren (RB 71), which ensures the proper coordination of the monks' efforts.

24. Ep 68.4; SBOp 7:168; James 99.

25. SC 84.4; SBOp 2:305; CF 40:191. A more complete treatment of Bernard's teaching on simplicity can be found in *Spiritual Teachings,* pp.

165–71. See, too, Michael Casey, "The Meaning of Poverty for Bernard of Clairvaux," *CSQ* 33 (1998) 427–38.

26. Apo 10.24; SBOp 3:101; CF 1:59. See also I Nov 2.2; SBOp 5:308; Luddy 2:350.

27. Apo 12.28; SBOp 3:104; CF 1:63.

28. Ep 398.2–3; SBOp 8:378; James 502.

29. Asspt 3.7; SBOp 5:243; Luddy 3:244.

30. Ep 87.8; SBOp 7:229; James 133.

31. Ep 345.1; SBOp 8:287; James 458.

32. Pent 3.8; SBOp 5:176; CF 53:86.

33. See Dil, prol.; SBOp 3:119; CF 13:91.

34. See RB 31.

35. SC 57.10; SBOp 2:125; CF 31:104–5.

36. SC 57.11; SBOp 2:125–26; CF 105.

37. SC 57.11; SBOp 2:126; CF 31:105–6. For a more complete discussion of Bernard's teaching on contemplation, see *Spiritual Teachings*, pp. 215–49.

38. Asspt 3.1; SBOp 5:239; Luddy 3:236.

39. See Asspt 3.2; SBOp 5:239; Luddy 3:238.

40. Hum 16.44; SBOp 3:50; CF 13:72.

41. SC 26.7; SBOp 1:175; CF 7:65–66.

42. SC 26.7; SBOp 1:175; CF 7:66. Quoted more fully below, pp. 59–60. Another activity in which some of the monks at Clairvaux participated was keeping notes on Bernard's talks. See Ep 18.5; SBOp 7:69; James 54.

43. SC 26.7; SBOp 1:175–76; CF 7:66. An earlier version of this section may be found in my "Bernard of Clairvaux's Abbot: Both Daniel and Noah," in Francis R. Swietek and John R. Sommerfeldt (eds.), Studiosorum speculum: *Studies in Honor of Louis J. Lekai, O.Cist.*, CS 141 (Kalamazoo, Michigan: Cistercian Publications, 1993), pp. 355–62.

44. Abb 1; SBOp 5:289; Luddy 3:307.

45. See Mor 9.33; SBOp 7:127–28. Though of the order of prelates, abbots must not "claim the pontifical insignia for themselves, using miter, ring, and sandals." Mor 9.36; SBOp 7:130.

46. Abb 6; SBOp 5:292–93; Luddy 3:312.

47. See SC 24.1; SBOp 1:151; CF 7:42.

48. SC 26.6; SBOp 1:174; CF 7:65.

49. SC 41.5; SBOp 2:31; CF 7:208.

50. SC 42.2; SBOp 2:34; CF 7:211–12. See also SC 42.4–5; SBOp 2:35–36; CF 7:212–14.

51. SC 10.1; SBOp 1:47; CF 4:61.

52. SC 10.2; SBOp 1:47; CF 4:61–62. See also I Sent 9 (SBOp 6/2:9; CF 55:120) and II Sent 168 (SBOp 6/2:55; CF 55:175).

53. Ep 115.1; SBOp 7:294; James 179. Bernard's hesitancy regarding the eremetical life is discussed by Thomas Renna in "The Wilderness and the Cistercians," *CSQ* 30 (1995) 185.

54. Ep 73.2; SBOp 1:180; James 107. See also I Sent 21; SBOp 6/2:15; CF 55:126.

55. SC 52.7; SBOp 2:94–95; CF 31:56.

56. See Apo 30; SBOp 3:106–7; CF 1:67.

57. SC 22.2; SBOp 1:130; CF 7:15.

58. SC 22.3; SBOp 1:130–31; CF 7:15–16. See also Dil 27; SBOp 3:142–43; CF 13:119. See, too, my "Bernard of Clairvaux as Sermon Writer and Sentence Speaker," the introduction to Bernard of Clairvaux, *The Sentences,* trans. Francis R. Swietek, in CF 55:105–14.

59. Hum, praef.; SBOp 3:16; CF 13:28.

60. What follows is a condensation of my treatment of the question in *Spiritual Teachings,* pp. 154–57 and 248–49. Some relevant passages not cited there include: SC 23.1 (SBOp 1:138–39; CF 7:26), SC 41.6 (SBOp 2:32; CF 7:208), SC 50.5 (SBOp 2:81; CF 31:34–35), SC 60.9 (SBOp 2:147; CF 31:138), Ep 82.1–2 (SBOp 7:214–16; James 121–22), Hum 10.29 (SBOp 3:39; CF 13:58), and QH 11.11 (SBOp 4:456; CF 25:211).

61. SC 23.2; SBOp 1:139; CF 7:26.

62. See PP 1.2; SBOp 5:189; CF 53:100. See also SC 8.7; SBOp 1:40; CF 4:50–51.

63. SC 58.1–2; SBOp 2:127–28; CF 31:108–9.

III. The Clerical Order of Noah

1. And, by extension, all the clergy engaged in an active, pastoral ministry. For example, Bernard's admonitions to Oger, a canon regular (Ep 87.3 and 5; SBOp 7:226–27; James 131–32), are virtually identical to those directed to Thursten, archbishop of York (Ep 319.1–2; SBOp 8:252; James 244). The link is their common "care of souls." For Bernard's teaching on the clergy, see Bede Lackner, "The Priestly Ideal of Saint Bernard," *The American Ecclesiastical Review* 140 (1959) 237–44; J. S. Maddux, "St. Bernard as Hagiographer," *Cîteaux* 27 (1976) 85–108; and Thomas Renna, "St Bernard's View of the Episcopacy in Historical Perspective, 400–1150," *CSQ*

15 (1980) 39–49. A useful table of the bishops with whom Bernard had contact is offered by Henry-Bernard de Warren's, "Bernard et l'épiscopat," in *Bernard de Clairvaux,* pp. 627–47.

2. See above, p. 6.

3. Abb 6; SBOp 5:292; Luddy 3:311.

4. Abb 6; SBOp 5:292; Luddy 3:311.

5. SC 25.2; SBOp 1:163; CF 7:51.

6. SC 25.2; SBOp 1:163–64; CF 7:51.

7. SC 23.2; SBOp 1:140; CF 7:27.

8. SC 85.13; SBOp 2:315; CF 40:209.

9. SC 9.8; SBOp 1:47; CF 4:59.

10. SC 9.9; SBOp 1:47; CF 4:59–60.

11. See Ep 238.2; SBOp 8:116–17; James 278.

12. Csi 1.5.6; SBOp 3:400; CF 37:33–34.

13. SC 18.3; SBOp 1:104; CF 4:134.

14. SC 18.3; SBOp 1:104; CF 4:134.

15. See Leclercq, "Saint Bernard on the Church," p. 286.

16. Mor 10–11; SBOp 7:108–9. As teachers and mediators, the clergy can confidently commit themselves to their own teachers and mediators, Peter and Paul. See PP 1.1; SBOp 5:188; CF 53:100.

17. Csi 2.6.13; SBOp 3:420; CF 37:62. See also I Sent 11 (SBOp 6/2:10; CF 55:120), II Sent 69 (SBOp 6/2:39; CF 55:156), and Div 100 (SBOp 6/1:367).

18. Csi 4.2.3; SBOp 3:451; CF 37:113. See III Sent 112 (SBOp 6/2:195; CF 55:120) and III Sent 118 (SBOp 6/2:213; CF 55:393–94).

19. See SC 77.5; SBOp 2:264; CF 40:125–26.

20. Csi 2.6.9; SBOp 3:416–17; CF 37:56–57. See Ep 238.6; SBOp 8:119; James 279.

21. Csi 3.1.2; SBOp 3:432; CF 37:80–81. See also Csi 2.6.11; SBOp 3:418; CF 37:59.

22. Csi 4.2.2; SBOp 3:450; CF 37:112.

23. SC 77.3; SBOp 2:263; CF 40:123.

24. Csi 3.3.13; SBOp 3:439; CF 37:93.

25. SC 29.6; SBOp 1:207; CF 7:107.

26. SC 76.9; SBOp 2:259; CF 40:117. In her *The Boundaries of Charity* (p. 2), Martha G. Newman writes that Bernard and the other early Cistercian leaders "worked to create a virtuous and moral clergy that would view its authority as a ministry, encourage the repentance and interior reform of the laity, and repair the social fabric."

27. SC 76.9; SBOp 2:259; CF 40:117–18.

28. SC 76.5; SBOp 2:259; CF 40:118.

29. SC 76.9; SBOp 2:259–60; CF 40:118. See SC 10.3 (SBOp 1:49–50; CF 4:62–63) and III Sent 116 (SBOp 6/2:210; CF 55:389) for biting descriptions of those clergy who do not respond to the demands of their ministry.

30. See SC 41.6; SBOp 2:32; CF 7:208.

31. See Csi 4.3.6; SBOp 3:454; CF 37:117. See also III Sent 66; SBOp 6/2:100; CF 55:237.

32. SC 76.7; SBOp 2:258; CF 40:115.

33. JB 11; SBOp 5:183; CF 53:95.

34. JB 4; SBOp 5:178; CF 53:90.

35. SC 76.9; SBOp 2:260; CF 40:119.

36. Csi 4.4.12; SBOp 3:458; CF 37:124.

37. Ep 213; SBOp 8:73; James 354.

38. V Mal 18.42; SBOp 3:347–48; CF 10:56.

39. V Mal 18.42; SBOp 3:348; CF 10:56–57.

40. SC 46.2; SBOp 2:56–57; CF 7:241–42.

41. SC 46.2; SBOp 2:57; CF 7:242. The power of bishops is given them only to fulfill their responsibilities. See Ep 256.2 (SBOp 8:164; James 471) and PP 1.2 (SBOp 5:189; CF 53:101). Their power is real; preaching may be done only with their authority (Ep 365.2; SBOp 8:321; James 465). The power of the bishop comes to him from his office (Ep 188.2; SBOp 8:11; James 316) and is independent of his virtue. See Mor 3.10 (SBOp 7:108), Miss 3.11 (SBOp 4:44; CF 18:42), and SC 66.11 (SBOp 2:185–86; CF 31:202–3). Nevertheless, bishops, and all the clergy, must be virtuous to discharge their office properly; see below, pp. 37–39.

42. See Csi 3.5.19; SBOp 3:446; CF 37:104. See also III Sent 112; SBOp 6/2:194, n. 5; CF 55:369–70, n. 138.

43. Csi 4.7.23; SBOp 3:465–66; CF 37:137. Bernard's admonition is a reflection of what he believes to be an unjust reality: the unwarranted realignment of ecclesiastical jurisdictions by the pope. See Bede Lackner, "Saint Bernard: On Bishops and Rome," *The American Benedictine Review* 40 (1989) 380–82. The fullness of power is the pope's, but he must use it justly (Csi 3.4.14; SBOp 3:442; CF 37:97–98). Bernard's teaching on the power of the pope, its nature and its sources, has been hotly debated. I think the debate is important but not relevant to this discussion. A few of the great number of comments on this subject can be consulted in Bernard Jacqueline, "Episcopat et papauté chez Saint Bernard de Clairvaux," *Coll*

34 (1972) 218–29; Elizabeth T. Kennan, "Antithesis and Argument in the *De consideratione*," in M. Basil Pennington (ed.), *Bernard of Clairvaux: Studies Presented to Dom Jean Leclercq*, CS 23 (Washington, D.C.: Cistercian Publications, 1973), pp. 91–109; Kennan, "The 'De consideratione,'" pp. 73–115; Richard Ver Bust, "Papal Ministry: A Source of Theology, Bernard of Clairvaux's Letters," in E. Rozanne Elder (ed.), *Heaven on Earth: Studies in Medieval Cistercian History, IX*, CS 68 (Kalamazoo, Michigan: Cistercian Publications, 1983), pp. 55–61; and Hayden V. White, "The Gregorian Ideal and Saint Bernard of Clairvaux," *Journal of the History of Ideas* 21 (1960) 321–48. I have taken issue with White's interpretation in "Charismatic and Gregorian Leadership in the Thought of Bernard of Clairvaux," in *Bernard of Clairvaux: Studies Presented to Dom Jean Leclercq*, pp. 73–90. A good summary of Bernard's position on the papacy can be found in Walter H. Principe, "Monastic, Episcopal, and Apologetic Theology of the Papacy, 1150–1250," in Christopher Ryan (ed.), *The Religious Roles of the Papacy: Ideals and Realities, 1150–1300*, Papers in Mediaeval Studies 8 (Toronto: Pontifical Institute of Mediaeval Studies, 1989), pp. 118–29.

44. Csi 4.2.2; SBOp 3:449; CF 37:110–11.

45. See Ep 348.3; SBOp 8:293; James 333.

46. See Ep 180; SBOp 7:402; James 301.

47. JB 9; SBOp 5:182; CF 53:94.

48. Ep 358; SBOp 8:303; James 374.

49. V Mal 27.59; SBOp 3:363; CF 10:74. Bernard does not criticize bishops' involvement in feudal relationships when that involvement is in the cause of peace and justice (see Ep 39.4; SBOp 7:98; James 74).

50. See V Mal 27.60; SBOp 3:363; CF 10:75.

51. See Csi 4.7.23; SBOp 3:466; CF 37:138.

52. Csi 4.6.20; SBOp 3:464; CF 37:134.

53. V Mal 8.16; SBOp 3:325–26; CF 10:34.

54. Tpl 12.30; SBOp 3:238; CF 19:165. Bernard is speaking of sacramental confession here, a relatively rare use of "confession" for him. Still more unusual is Bernard's reference to confession, confirmation, and matrimony in V Mal 3.7; SBOp 3:316; CF 10:22. For a discussion of Bernard's teaching on confession, which goes far beyond the sacrament, see J. Leclercq, "St Bernard on Confession," *CSQ* 4 (1969) 199–212.

55. Ep 173; SBOp 7:387; James 287.

56. Ep 257.2; SBOp 8:166; James 412.

57. Ep 342.2; SBOp 8:285; James 457.

58. Ep 95; SBOp 7:245; James 240. The poor, in this case, are needy monks.

59. Ep 189.5; SBOp 8:16; James 320. Those predecessors Bernard sees as having refuted, by their preaching, the heresies of "Arius, Pelagius, and others like them." See Par 6; SBOp 6/2:294; CF 55:83–84.

60. Par 6; SBOp 6/2:287; CF 55:73.

61. SC 65.1; SBOp 2:172; CF 31:180. Bernard gives an example of such a public refutation in V Mal 25.57; SBOp 3:360; CF 10:71.

62. SC 64.8; SBOp 2:170; CF 31:175.

63. Csi 4.7.23; SBOp 3:466; CF 37:137–38.

64. See Ep 230; SBOp 8:100; James 299–300.

65. Csi 2.6.12; SBOp 3:419; CF 37:25–26. Bernard describes the burdens of the clergy in Csi 1.1.1 (SBOp 3:394–95; CF 37:25–26) and Csi 1.4.5 (SBOp 3:398–99; CF 37:31–32).

IV. Noah's Many Virtues

1. Vict 2.3; SBOp 6/1:35; Luddy 3:114.

2. Mor 2.4; SBOp 7:104.

3. SC 46.3; SBOp 2:57; CF 7:242.

4. Ep 249; SBOp 8:144; James 400.

5. See Abb 6; SBOp 5:293; Luddy 3:313. See, too, II Sent 34; SBOp 6/2:33; CF 55:149–50.

6. See Ep 28.1; SBOp 7:81; James 62.

7. Ep 27; SBOp 7:80; James 62.

8. PP 1.2; SBOp 5:189; CF 53:101. See III Sent 13; SBOp 6/2:72; CF 55:199.

9. Csi 1.5.6; SBOp 3:400; CF 37:33.

10. For a discussion of Bernard's teaching on humility, see *Spiritual Teachings*, pp. 53–63.

11. Ep 392; SBOp 8:362; James 495. See also Ep 9 (SBOp 7:50; James 40–41) and Ep 27 (SBOp 7:80; James 62).

12. Ep 393.3; SBOp 8:367; James 296. See also Ep 372; SBOp 8:332–33; James 484–85.

13. For a more complete discussion of meditation, see *Spiritual Teachings*, pp. 66–77.

14. Mor 2.5; SBOp 7:105.

15. V Mal 14.32; SBOp 3:339; CF 10:48.

16. Mal 4; SBOp 6/1:53; CF 10:110.

17. Csi 2.3.6; SBOp 3:414; CF 37:52.

18. Csi 2.3.6; SBOp 3:414; CF 37:52.

19. Csi 2.4.7; SBOp 3:415; CF 37:54.

20. See Csi 3, *passim;* SBOp 3:431–48; CF 37:79–107.

21. See Csi 4, *passim;* SBOp 3:448–66; CF 37:109–38.

22. See Csi 5, *passim;* SBOp 3:467–93; CF 37:139–79.

23. Csi 2.7.14; SBOp 3:422; CF 37:64.

24. Ep 238.7; SBOp 8:119; James 280.

25. SC 62.4; SBOp 2:157; CF 31:154. For the cleric's simplicity, see S Mal 1 (SBOp 6/1:51; CF 10:107–8) and Ep 362.2 (SBOp 8:310; James 387).

26. SC 62.3; SBOp 2:157; CF 31:154.

27. SC 18.6; SBOp 1:107–8; CF 4:138. For a more complete description of Bernard's teaching on love, see *Spiritual Teachings,* pp. 89–120.

28. See Abb 6; SBOp 5:292; Luddy 3:312.

29. SC 76.8; SBOp 2:259; CF 40:117. See III Sent 112; SBOp 6/2:193–94; CF 55:369.

30. Csi 1.2.3; SBOp 3:396; CF 37:27.

31. SC 9.10; SBOp 1:48; CF 4:60. See III Sent 121; SBOp 6/2:226; CF 55:417.

32. See Ep 372; SBOp 8:333; James 485.

33. See SC 76.9; SBOp 2:260; CF 40:118.

34. See Csi 1.9.12; SBOp 3:407–8; CF 37:43.

35. Mor 13; SBOp 7:111.

36. SC 18.2; SBOp 1:104; CF 4:134.

37. See SC 23.8; SBOp 1:144; CF 7:32. The models Bernard presents are Peter and Paul. See SC 30.8; SBOp 1:215; CF 7:118–19. The vice of ambition seems to be the opposite of the virtue of self-giving in the cleric's ministry. See Csi 3.1.5; SBOp 3:434; CF 37:84–85.

38. Ep 23.2–3; SBOp 7:74–75; James 58. The importance to Bernard of his teaching on clerical poverty is indicated by the number of times he enunciates it with negative examples. See SC 23.12 (SBOp 1:146–47; CF 7:36), SC 33.15 (SBOp 1:244; CF 7:157–58), SC 41.6 (SBOp 2:32; CF 7:208), Csi 2.6.10 (SBOp 3:417; CF 37:57), Csi 3.5.19 (SBOp 3:446; CF 37:105), Csi 4.3.6 (SBOp 3:453–54; CF 37:117), Conv 14.26 (SBOp 4:101; CF 25:62), Mor 2.7 (SBOp 7:106–7), and QH 6.7 (SBOp 4:410; CF 25:149).

39. Csi 4.4.12; SBOp 3:458; CF 37:124.

40. Conv 16.29; SBOp 4:104–5; CF 25:65–66.

41. Ep 238.6; SBOp 8:118; James 279.

42. See Mart 15; SBOp 5:409; Luddy 3:19–20.

43. V Mal, *praef.*; SBOp 3:308; CF 10:12.

44. V Mal 19.43; SBOp 3:348–49; CF 10:57–58. See Mal 6; SBOp 5:421; CF 10:102.

45. Ep 135; SBOp 7:331; James 205.

46. Conv 20.36; SBOp 4:113; CF 25:74. On the relationship between continence, enjoined on all, and celibacy, necessary for those who choose monastic or clerical life, see *Spiritual Teachings,* pp. 161–63.

47. Mor 3.8; SBOp 7:107.

48. Mor 3.9; SBOp 7:108.

49. See Maddux, "St. Bernard as Hagiographer," p. 90.

50. Mor 4.13; SBOp 7:111.

51. SC 62.8; SBOp 2:160; CF 31:159.

52. Csi 4.4.12; SBOp 3:457–58; CF 37:124.

53. See, for example, Mart 1; SBOp 5:399; Luddy 3:2.

54. Ep 392; SBOp 8:363; James 496.

55. Csi 2.13.22; SBOp 3:429; CF 37:76.

56. Ep 362.2; SBOp 8:310; James 387.

57. Ep 392; SBOp 8:361–62; James 495.

58. Csi 2.6.9; SBOp 3:417; CF 37:57.

59. V Mal 14.34; SBOp 3:340; CF 10:49.

60. Csi 1.8.10; SBOp 3:405; CF 37:39–40.

61. Ep 257.1; SBOp 8:165–66; James 412.

62. Ep 26; SBOp 7:79; James 61. See III Sent 112; SBOp 6/2:193; CF 55:368–69.

63. Csi 3.5.19; SBOp 3:447; CF 37:105.

64. See Csi 1.8.9; SBOp 3:404–5; CF 37:38–39.

65. Csi 1.9.12; SBOp 3:407; CF 37:43.

66. Ep 25.2; SBOp 7:79; James 61.

67. Mart 14; SBOp 5:409; Luddy 3:18.

68. SC 58.3; SBOp 2:128; CF 31:109–10.

69. SC 58.3; SBOp 2:128–29; CF 31:110.

70. Mal 3; SBOp 5:419; CF 10:99. On the clergy as men of prayer, see Ep 201.3; SBOp 8:61; James 340.

71. Conv 22.40; SBOp 4:115–16; CF 25:78–79.

72. Csi 4.4.12; SBOp 3:457; CF 37:123–24.

73. They also serve as the eyes (bishops), nose (archdeacons), ears (deacons), and mouth and tongue (priests and deacons) of the body that is the Church. See III Sent 118; SBOp 6/2:213–14; CF 55:393–94.

V. The Lay Order of Job

1. Div 9.3; SBOp 6/1:119. For a survey of Bernard's teaching on the laity, see Hans Wolter, "Bernhard von Clairvaux und die Laien: Aussagen der monastischen Theologie über Ort und Berufung des Laien in der erlösten Welt," *Scholastik* 34 (1959) 161–89. For Bernard's teaching on married life, see my "Bernard of Clairvaux on Love and Marriage," *CSQ* 30 (1995) 141–46.

2. Miss 1.5; SBOp 4:17; CF 18:9.

3. Pre 16.48; SBOp 3:286; CF 1:141. See III Sent 17; SBOp 6/2:75; CF 55:202–3.

4. SC 66.5; SBOp 2:181–82; CF 31:196.

5. Ep 7.4; SBOp 7:34; James 28.

6. Ep 7.2; SBOp 7:32; James 27.

7. Ep 421; SBOp 8:405; James 514. See Jean Leclercq, *Women and Saint Bernard of Clairvaux*, trans. Marie-Bernard Saïd, CS 104 (Kalamazoo, Michigan: Cistercian Publications, 1989), pp. 22 and 27.

8. Ep 119; SBOp 7:299; James 183. Jean Leclercq comments: "It would be difficult to combine in fewer words married love and total love for Christ. Husband and wife are, in the manner unique to their married state, specialists of bridal union with Christ." Leclercq, "Does St Bernard Have a Specific Message for Nuns?" in John A. Nichols and Lillian Thomas Shank (eds.), *Medieval Religious Women*, I, *Distant Echoes*, CS 71 (Kalamazoo, Michigan: Cistercian Publications Inc., 1984), p. 274. See also Div 27.3; SBOp 6/1:199.

9. Pre 15.42; SBOp 3:282; CF 1:137.

10. SC 66.3; SBOp 2:179; CF 31:193.

11. See SC 66.4; SBOp 2:181; CF 31:195.

12. Div 80.1; SBOp 6/1:320. See SC 8.9; SBOp 1:41; CF 4:52. Of course, Bernard teaches that "marriage is the only condition which justifies sexual intercourse [see Mt 19:10]." SC 66.1; SBOp 2:179; CF 31:191.

13. Dil 7.17; SBOp 3:133–34; CF 13:110. See *Spiritual Teachings*, pp. 95–96.

14. Gra 2.3–4; SBOp 3:168; CF 19:58. See *Spiritual Teachings*, pp. 10 and 96.

15. SC 26.10; SBOp 1:178; CF 7:69. See *Spiritual Teachings*, pp. 107–11.

16. Jean Leclercq, *Monks on Marriage: A Twelfth-Century View* (New York: The Seabury Press, 1982), p. 79.

17. SC 85.12; SBOp 2:315; CF 40:208–9.

18. SC 84.6; SBOp 2:306; CF 40:192–93.

19. SC 83.3; SBOp 2:299; CF 40:182.

20. See SC 81.1; SBOp 2:284; CF 40:157–58. See also Leclercq, *Monks on Marriage*, p. 78.

21. SC 7.2; SBOp 1:31–32; CF 4:39.

22. SC 66.7; SBOp 2:182–83; CF 31:198.

23. SC 66.10; SBOp 2:185; CF 31:201–2.

24. Ep 300; SBOp 8:216; James 437.

25. Pre 18.56; SBOp 3:290; CF 1:146.

26. SC 83.5–6; SBOp 2:301–2; CF 40:185–86.

27. Leclercq, *Monks on Marriage*, p. 79.

28. Leclercq, *Monks on Marriage*, pp. 79 and 86. Bernard also sees marriage, this time between Adam and Eve, as an image of the union between body and soul. See QH 10.3; SBOp 4:444–45; CF 25:195.

29. Ep 131.1; SBOp 7:327; James 208.

30. Ep 363.5; SBOp 8:315; James 462.

31. Bermard does not even condemn profits from money-lending. See Ep 201.2, SBOp 8:60; James 339.

32. Par 7; SBOp 6/2:295; CF 55:89.

33. Par 7; SBOp 6/2:302; CF 55:99.

34. Ep 314; SBOp 8:246; James 206.

35. Csi 2.6.10; SBOp 3:417–18; CF 37:58. See III Sent 109; SBOp 6/2:181; CF 55:350.

36. Dil 4.11; SBOp 3:128; CF 13:103. See Dil 7.18; SBOp 3:134; CF 13:111.

37. Conv 8.14; SBOp 4:88–89; CF 25:49.

38. Dil 4.11; SBOp 3:128; CF 13:104.

39. Dil 4.11; SBOp 3:128–29; CF 13:104.

40. Dil 7.19; SBOp 3:135; CF 13:112.

41. SC 21.7; SBOp 1:126; CF 7:9.

42. SC 21.7; SBOp 1:126; CF 7:9.

43. Ep 95; SBOp 7:245; James 240.

44. Ep 421; SBOp 8:405; James 514.

45. Ep 133; SBOp 7:329; James 207.

46. Ep 129.2; SBOp 7:323; James 200–201.

47. Ep 243.3; SBOp 8:131; James 392.

48. See below, pp. 109–13.

49. III Sent 118; SBOp 6/2:215; CF 55:396.

50. SC 26.7; SBOp 1:175; CF 7:66.

51. See Miss 1.5; SBOp 4:17; CF 18:9.

VI. Job's Ministry of Governance

1. See Jean Richard, "Le milieu familial," in *Bernard de Clairvaux,* pp. 3–15. For an analytical listing of those rulers with whom Bernard corresponded, see Henry-Bernard de Warren, "Bernard, les princes et la société féodal," in *Bernard de Clairvaux,* pp. 649–57. Much of the material in the following two sections has appeared, in an earlier form, in my "Vassals of the Lord and Ministers of God," *CSQ* 29 (1994) 55–60.

2. As Bruno Scott James points out, Bernard was content to work within the political framework of his time. See Bruno S. James, *Saint Bernard of Clairvaux: An Essay in Biography* (London: Hodder & Stoughton, 1957), p. 87.

3. Ded 5.9; SBOp 5:395; Luddy 2:428.

4. Ep 139.1; SBOp 7:335; James 210.

5. Ep 244.1; SBOp 8:134; James 394. Knights are the chest, back, arms, and hands of the Church, as bishops are her eyes. See III Sent 118; SBOp 6/2:214; CF 55:395.

6. Ep 244.1; SBOp 8:134–35; James 394.

7. Ep 244.3; SBOp 8:135; James 395.

8. See Ep 244.3; SBOp 8:135; James 395.

9. See Ep 97.1; SBOp 7:247; James 143.

10. See Ep 170.1–2 (SBOp 7:383–84; James 257–58) and Ep 183 (SBOp 8:3; James 304–5).

11. Ep 92; SBOp 7:241; James 142.

12. Ep 497; SBOp 8:454; James 75.

13. Ep 255.1; SBOp 8:161; James 203.

14. Ep 449; SBOp 8:427; James 286.

15. Ep 279; SBOp 8:191; James 429. For this and the following section, see William O. Paulsell, "Saint Bernard on the Duties of the Christian Prince," in *Studies in Medieval Cistercian History, II,* pp. 63–74.

16. Ep 39.1; SBOp 7:97; James 73.

17. Ep 217; SBOp 8:77; James 362.

18. See Ep 372.2 (SBOp 8:341; James 476), Ep 301.1 (SBOp 8:218; James 438), and Ep 455 (SBOp 8:430–31; James 438–39).

19. Ep 220.1; SBOp 8:82–83; James 363.

20. See Ep 223.2 (SBOp 8:90; James 369), Ep 221.4 (SBOp 8:85–86; James 365–66), Ep 299 (SBOp 8:215; James 436), Ep 375 (SBOp 8:338; James 486–87), Ep 219.3 (SBOp 8:81; James 360), and V Mal 4.9 (SBOp 3:319; CF 10:26).

21. See Ep 130 (SBOp 7:325; James 202), Ep 140 (SBOp 7:337; James 211), and Ep 348.1 (SBOp 8:292; James 332). See Helene Wieruszowski, "Roger II of Sicily, *Rex-Tyrannus,* in Twelfth-Century Political Thought," *Speculum* 38 (1963) 46–78, especially pp. 53–54 and 57–59.

22. Ep 206; SBOp 8:65; James 345. For Bernard's correspondence with Melisande and other women of the time, see Leclercq, *Women and Saint Bernard of Clairvaux, passim.* See also Edith Russel, "Bernard et les dames de son temps," in *Bernard de Clairvaux,* pp. 411–25.

23. Ep 289.2; SBOp 8:206; James 348.

24. See Ep 207; SBOp 8:66; James 349.

25. Ep 299; SBOp 8:215; James 436.

26. Ep 39.2; SBOp 7:98; James 73.

27. Ep 39.3; SBOp 7:98; James 73–74. Bernard also urges Adelaide, queen of France and wife of Louis VI, to do her duty to defend a subject unjustly condemned to exile (Ep 511; SBOp 8:470).

28. Ep 37.1–2; SBOp 7:95; James 71–72.

29. See Ep 303; SBOp 8:220; James 439.

30. See Ep 170.2; SBOp 7:384; James 258.

31. See Ep 39.4; SBOp 7:98; James 74.

32. Ep 533; SBOp 8:498; James 267.

33. Ep 282.1; SBOp 8:196; James 427.

34. See Ep 534; SBOp 8:499; James 268.

35. See Ep 534; SBOp 8:499; James 267.

36. Ep 219.3; SBOp 8:81; James 361.

37. See Ep 316; SBOp 8:249; James 448.

38. See Ep 271; SBOp 8:181; James 419.

39. See Ep 224.3; SBOp 8:92; James 370–71.

40. See Ep 140; SBOp 7:337; James 211. See Jean Leclercq, "Saint Bernard's Attitude Toward War," in *Studies in Medieval Cistercian History, II,* p. 4. Some of the material in this section has appeared, in an earlier form, in my "The Bernardine Reform and the Crusading Spirit," *The Catholic Historical Review* 86 (2000) 567–78.

41. Ep 83.2; SBOp 7:217; James 123.

42. Ep 226.1; SBOp 8:95; James 372.

43. Ep 170.3; SBOp 7:384; James 259.

44. Ep 206; SBOp 8:65; James 345.

45. Ep 377.1; SBOp 8:340–41; James 475.

46. Ep 129.3; SBOp 7:324; James 201.

47. Ep 138; SBOp 7:334; James 209.

48. Tpl 3.5; SBOp 3:217–18; CF 19:135. Although this and the following quotations are addressed to the Knights Templar, they are, I believe, applicable to all who follow the profession of arms. As Thomas Renna has written, Bernard's position is that "to live in the spirit of the crusade is within the reach of all knights." See "Early Cistercian Attitudes Toward War in Historical Perspective," *Cîteaux* 31 (1980) 126.

49. Tpl 5.9; SBOp 3:222; CF 19:142.

50. Tpl 3.4; SBOp 3:217; CF 19:134.

51. See Tpl 3.4; SBOp 3:217; CF 19:134. I am indebted to Jean Leclercq for recognition of this play on words. See "Saint Bernard's Attitude Toward War," p. 23.

52. Ep 120; SBOp 7:301; James 184.

53. Ep 220.2; SBOp 8:83; James 363–64.

54. Ep 221.1; SBOp 8:84; James 364.

55. Tpl 2.3; SBOp 3:216; CF 19:132–33.

56. Ep 137; SBOp 7:333; James 207.

57. See Ep 222.4; SBOp 8:88; James 367–68.

58. Leclercq, "Saint Bernard's Attitude Toward War," p. 36.

59. Ep 363.1; SBOp 8:312; James 461.

60. See SBOp 8:311, n. 1.

61. Ep 363; SBOp 8:311.

62. Csi 2.1.1; SBOp 3:411; CF 37:49.

63. Ep 458.3; SBOp 8:435; James 464.

64. Ep 363.7; SBOp 8:316–17; James 463.

65. Tpl 3.4; SBOp 3:217; CF 19:135.

66. This moderate position seems flatly contradicted by Bernard's letter to the crusaders about to attack the Wends, a Slavic people of central Europe. Bernard writes: "I forbid you to enter into a treaty with them—in any way or for any reason whatsoever: not for money, not for tribute, until, with God's help, either their religious observances or their nation be destroyed" (Ep 457; SBOp 8:433; James 467). Two factors explain and, perhaps, mitigate Bernard's seeming severity.

First, Bernard fears the Wends will attack the crusaders' line of march to the East and thus "close the road to Jerusalem." But only if the Wends do indeed unjustly attack those who have "taken the sign of salvation" should they, in turn, be attacked (Ep 457; SBOp 8:433; James 467).

Second, one must take account of Hans Dietrich Kahl's argument, based on a wide variety of sources, that the "destruction" of the Wends could be accomplished as well by baptism as by physical force, as Bernard saw it. See Kahl's "Crusade Eschatology as Seen by St. Bernard in the Years 1146 to 1148," in Michael Gervers (ed.), *The Second Crusade and the Cistercians* (New York: St. Martin's Press, 1992), p. 37.

67. It is difficult to reconcile Bernard's words, as quoted in this paragraph, with Eoin de Bhaldraithe's assertion that "for Bernard the Muslims were infidels and were to be killed...." See his "Jean Leclercq's Attitude Toward War," in E. Rozanne Elder (ed.), *The Joy of Learning and the Love of God: Studies in Honor of Jean Leclercq*, CS 160 (Kalamazoo, Michigan; Spencer, Massachusetts: Cistercian Publications, 1995), p. 218. This entire article is characterized by moral outrage directed at Bernard's position on warfare and at the empathic attempts of Leclercq to present and analyze it.

68. Tpl 3.5–6; SBOp 3:218–19; CF 19:135–36.

69. Ep 350; SBOp 8:294; James 357.

70. See Ep 363.3–4; SBOp 8:313–14; James 461. See also Ep 458.2; SBOp 8:435; James 463–64.

71. Renna, "Early Cistercian Attitudes Toward War," p. 125.

72. Ep 364.1; SBOp 8:318; James 469.

73. Ep 380; SBOp 8:344; James 478.

74. Ep 363.5; SBOp 8:314–15; James 462.

75. Hans-Dietrich Kahl would add another reason for—or, perhaps, another dimension to—Bernard's crusade preaching. Kahl sees that preaching as an expression of Bernard's eschatological expectations. See Kahl's "Crusade Eschatology," pp. 35–47. A fuller treatment of this theme can be found in Kahl's "Die Kreuzzugseschatologie Bernhards von Clairvaux und ihre missionsgeschichtliche Auswirkung," in Dieter R. Bauer and Gotthard Fuchs (eds.), *Bernhard von Clairvaux und der Beginn der Moderne* (Innsbruck, Wien: Tyrolia-Verlag, 1996), pp. 262–315. Kahl bases his argument in part on Bernard McGinn's article "Saint Bernard and Eschatology," in *Bernard of Clairvaux: Studies*, pp. 161–85. However, McGinn merely offers this eschatological explanation as a possibility. He states (on p. 182) that some passages "in Bernard's works may suggest that there was an eschatological dimension to his attitude towards the Crusades." Even if McGinn's suggestion and Kahl's assertion of this position are correct, I do not see that they conflict with Bernard's self-declared motives.

76. Csi 2.1.2; SBOp 3:412; CF 37:49.

77. See Csi 2.1.3; SBOp 3:412; CF 37:50.

78. Ep 288.1; SBOp 8:203–4; James 479.

79. Tpl 1.1; SBOp 3:214–15; CF 19:130. See Giles Constable, *The Reformation of the Twelfth Century*, p. 76. He writes: "The military orders represented one effort to institutionalize this ethos [of military saints and saintly knights], as did, on a broader scale, the crusades, which opened an almost automatic path to heaven for those who took the cross humbly and penitently and who died fighting the enemies of Christianity."

80. Ep 354; SBOp 8:298; James 346.

81. Tpl 4.7; SBOp 3:219; CF 19:138.

82. Tpl 4.7; SBOp 3:219–20; CF 19:138–39.

83. Tpl 4.8; SBOp 3:220–21; CF 19:139–40.

84. Tpl 4.8; SBOp 3:221; CF 19:140.

85. See *Spiritual Teachings*, p. 53.

86. See Ep 354; SBOp 8:297–98; James 346.

87. SC 83.1; SBOp 2:299; CF 40:181. See Leclercq, *Women and Saint Bernard of Clairvaux*, p. 163.

88. See Ep 113.1; SBOp 7:288; James 174.

89. Tpl 13.31; SBOp 3:239; CF 19:167. See Ep 371; SBOp 8:330; James 473.

90. See *Spiritual Teachings*, pp. 89–90.

91. Ep 497; SBOp 8:454; James 76.

92. See Ep 378; SBOp 8:342; James 477.

93. See Ep 516; SBOp 8:475; James 310. Some other letters on alms for needy monasteries are Ep 186 (SBOp 8:8–9; James 308), Ep 409 (SBOp 8:390; James 507–8), Ep 416 (SBOp 8:400–401; James 512–13), and Ep 513 (SBOp 8:472–73; James 310–11).

94. See *Spiritual Teachings*, pp. 97–98.

95. Ep 40; SBOp 7:99; James 74.

96. Ep 209; SBOp 8:68–69; James 350. See also Ep 41 (SBOp 7:99–100; James 74–75), Ep 207 (SBOp 8:66–67; James 348–49), and Ep 519 (SBOp 8:478–79; James 241–42).

97. See Ep 216; SBOp 8:76; James 362.

98. Ep 119; SBOp 7:299; James 183.

99. Ep 519; SBOp 8:478; James 242.

100. See Ep 137; SBOp 7:333; James 207. See also Ep 39.2–3; SBOp 7:98; James 73.

101. Ep 206; SBOp 8:65; James 345.

102. See Ep 350; SBOp 8:294; James 357.

103. Res 3.6; SBOp 5:109; Luddy 2:207.

104. Ep 175; SBOp 7:393; James 294.

105. Ep 38.2; SBOp 7:96; James 72.

106. Ep 38.2; SBOp 7:96–97; James 72–73. The same idea is expressed negatively in Bernard's attack on Count Theobald's long-standing enemy, King Louis VII. See Ep 224.3; SBOp 8:92; James 371.

107. Tpl 2.3; SBOp 3:216; CF 19:132. See Ep 458.5; SBOp 8:436; James 464.

108. See above, pp. 17–18, and *Spiritual Teachings*, pp. 165–71.

109. Ep 289.2; SBOp 8:206; James 347.

VII. The Dissidents

1. Hum 22.56; SBOp 3:54; CF 13:81.

2. Csi 3.1.4; SBOp 3:433–34; CF 37:83.

3. Ep 178.3; SBOp 7:399; James 298. The schismatics of this letter are not Greeks, but, I believe, the principle holds true, in Bernard's view, for all separated from what he believes is legitimate ecclesiastical authority.

4. See Csi 3.1.3; SBOp 3:43; CF 37:82.

5. See above, pp. 71–72.

6. A comprehensive treatment of the question is found in Jean Leclercq, "L'hérésie d'après les écrits de s. Bernard de Clairvaux," in W. Lourdaux and D. Verhelst (eds.), *The Concept of Heresy in the Middle Ages (11–13th C.): Proceedings of the International Conference, Louvain, May 13–16, 1973,* Mediaevalia Lovaniensis, Series 1, Studies 4 (Louvain: University Press; The Hague: Martinus Nijhoff, 1976), pp. 12–26.

7. Ep 241.1; SBOp 8:125; James 388.

8. Ep 241.1; SBOp 8:125–26; James 388. See also Csi 3.1.4; SBOp 3:434; CF 37:83.

9. SC 65.1; SBOp 2:172; CF 31:180.

10. See above, pp. 34–35.

11. SC 66.14; SBOp 2:188; CF 31:206.

12. SC 66.12; SBOp 2:186–87; CF 31:204.

13. SC 66.12; SBOp 2:187; CF 31:204.

14. SC 66.14; SBOp 2:187; CF 31:205. See Leclercq, "Saint Bernard's Attitude Toward War," pp. 18–20. As Leclercq remarks there (p. 19), Bernard does speak of "persecution" in his Ep 242.1 (SBOp 8:128; James 390), but he is using the term with a "precise juridical meaning...[which] referred to the prevention of wrong-doing and a subsequent coercion in favor of good conduct."

15. SC 64.8; SBOp 2:170; CF 31:175. See above, p. 35, where I have used this quotation in another context.

16. Ep 457; SBOp 8:433; James 467. As I noted above (pp. 146–47, n. 66), Hans-Dietrich Kahl argues, on the basis of comparison with other texts, that the destruction of which Bernard speaks can be by baptism as well as physical force. See Kahl's "Crusade Eschatology," p. 37.

17. Ep 457; SBOp 8:433; James 467.

18. Leclercq, *Bernard of Clairvaux and the Cistercian Spirit,* p. 64.

19. See SC 30.4; SBOp 1:212; CF 7:114–15.

20. Dil 3.7; SBOp 3:124; CF 13:99.

21. Csi 3.1.3; SBOp 3:433; CF 37:82.

22. See above, pp. 70–71.

23. See Tpl 7.13; SBOp 3:226; CF 19:149.

24. SC 14.1–2; SBOp 1:75–77; CF 4:97–99.

25. Ep 363.6–7; SBOp 8:316; James 462–63.

26. Csi 3.1.3; SBOp 3:433; CF 37:82.

27. SC 79.5; SBOp 2:275; CF 40:141–42.

28. The words are Jean Leclercq's. See *Women and Saint Bernard of Clairvaux,* p. 164.

29. Ep 365.2; SBOp 8:321; James 465.

30. Ep 365.2; SBOp 8:322; James 466.

31. Ep 365.2; SBOp 8:321–22; James 466.

VIII. Daniel, Noah, and Job: A Hierarchy?

1. See above, p. 12.

2. Hugh Feiss, "St Bernard's Theology of Baptism and the Monastic Life," *CSQ* 25 (1990) 85, citing Div 93.2; SBOp 6/1:349–51.

3. Feiss, p. 85.

4. Ep 103.1; SBOp 7:259–60; James 151.

5. Tpl 3.5; SBOp 3:218; CF 19:135.

6. "Epistemological and Social Hierarchies: A Potential Reconciliation of Some Inconsistencies in Bernard's Thought," *Cîteaux* 31 (1990) 85. This article (pp. 83–92 in *Cîteaux*) was reprinted in Marion Leathers Kuntz and Paul Grimley Kuntz (eds.), *Jacob's Ladder and the Tree of Life: Concepts of Hierarchy and the Great Chain of Being,* American University Studies, Series 5, Philosophy 14 (New York, Bern, Frankfurt am Main, Paris: Peter Lang, 1987), pp. 141–51.

7. *Spiritual Teachings,* p. 3.

8. See Fritegotto, pp. 72–73.

9. SC 27.6; SBOp 1:185; CF 7:79. See, too, SC 26.2; SBOp 1:170; CF 7:59. For other examples of apparently negative statements on the body, see *Spiritual Teachings*, pp. 3–5.

10. This I have attempted to do in *Spiritual Teachings*, pp. 5–6, 24–25, and 35–37.

11. QH 14.1; SBOp 4:469; CF 25:229.

12. See Dil 11.32; SBOp 3:146; CF 13:123–24.

13. To be philosophically correct, I should have written: "…an *onto-logical* factor which established them [the states of life] in a hierarchical relationship." But that would have betrayed Bernard still more miserably.

14. SC 62.1; SBOp 2:154–55; CF 31:149–51.

15. Apo 3.5; SBOp 3:84–85; CF 1:38. This passage is quoted in greater length above, p. 10. Speaking to monks (in III Sent 91; SBOp 6/2:141; CF 55:290) Bernard expresses the same idea, but negatively: "…And let no one in the cloister fall asleep or grow sluggish in sloth like a lazy and worthless servant [see Mt 25:26; Lk 19:22]. It is one's [way of] life that brings merit; one's place [in life] does not make one blessed."

16. See QH 7.10; SBOp 4:420; CF 25:161.

17. Pre 15.42–43; SBOp 3:282–83; CF 1:137.

18. Csi 3.4.15; SBOp 3:442; CF 37:98.

19. Ep 7.4; SBOp 7:33–34; James 28.

20. See *Spiritual Teachings*, pp. 183–93.

21. Ep 7.4; SBOp 7:34; James 28. See also Div 41.3; SBOp 6/1:246–47; Luddy 3:466.

22. SC 71.1; SBOp 2:215; CF 40:48–49.

23. See *Spiritual Teachings*, pp. 53–63.

24. See Miss 4.9; SBOp 4:55; CF 18:54–55.

25. See Miss 4.10; SBOp 4:55–56; CF 18:55–56.

26. SC 69.1; SBOp 2:202; CF 40:27. See II Sent 20; SBOp 6/2:29–30; CF 55:145.

27. Pre 3.7; SBOp 3:258; CF 1:110.

28. Ep 254.3; SBOp 8:158; James 410. The possibility of perfection is discussed in *Spiritual Teachings*, pp. 205–10.

29. See Apo 4.9; SBOp 3:89; CF 1:44; quoted above, p. 12.

30. Ep 105; SBOp 7:265; James 155.

31. Ep 112.1–2; SBOp 7:286–87; James 171–72.

32. Ep 515; SBOp 8:474; James 309.

33. For a discussion of Bernard as recruiter, see Marion Rissetto, "Fish for the Pond: The Recruitment Dynamic of Bernard of Clairvaux," *Word and*

Spirit: A Monastic Review 12 (1990) 148–61. In II Sent 21 (SBOp 6/2:30; CF 55:145–46), Bernard writes: "The trees [see Ps 95:12] are all the just.... Let each of them see to it, therefore, that he chooses for himself a well-watered spot, in which, in his season [see Ps 1:3], he can be productive and bear the fruit of life."

 34. See Ep 408 (SBOp 8:389; James 507) and Ep 442 (SBOp 8:420; James 518).

 35. See Ep 422; SBOp 8:406; James 515.

 36. See Ep 110; SBOp 7:282–83; James 169.

 37. See Ep 104 (SBOp 7:261–63; James 152–54), Ep 105 (SBOp 7:264–65; James 154–55), perhaps Ep 106 (SBOp 7:265–67; James 155–56), Ep 107 (SBOp 7:267–76; James 158–65), Ep 108 (SBOp 7:277–79; James 165–67), Ep 411 (SBOp 8:392–94; James 156–58), Ep 412 (SBOp 8:394–95; James 508–9), and Ep 415 (SBOp 8:398–99; James 511).

 38. See Ep 103; SBOp 7:259–60; James 151–52.

 39. See, for example, White, "The Gregorian Ideal," pp. 321–48. Some of this section is a treatment of texts also discussed in my article "The Intellectual Life According to Saint Bernard," *Cîteaux* 25 (1974) 249–56.

 40. *Fragmenta de vita et miraculis s. Bernardi,* 49, ed. Robert Lechat, in *Analecta Bollandiana* 50 (1932) 115–16. My translation is based, in part, on that by Martinus Cawley in *Bernard of Clairvaux: Early Biographies, II, By Geoffrey and Others* (Lafayette, Oregon: Guadalupe Translations, 1990), p. 8.

 41. *Fragmenta* 49; *Analecta Bollandiana,* 116; Cawley 8–9.

 42. Conv 19.32; SBOp 4:109; CF 25:69.

 43. Conv 19.32; SBOp 4:109; CF 25:69–70.

 44. Conv 19.32; SBOp 4:109; CF 25:70.

 45. Conv 19.32; SBOp 4:109–10; CF 35:70–71.

 46. Conv 30.34; SBOp 4:111; CF 25:72–73.

 47. See Conv 8.15; SBOp 4:89; CF 25:49–50.

 48. Conv 21.37; SBOp 4:113; CF 25:75.

 49. Ep 319.1–2; SBOp 8:252; James 244.

 50. See Conv 21.38; SBOp 4:114; CF 25:76.

 51. See Tpl 5.10; SBOp 3:223. See the section on conversion in *Spiritual Teachings,* pp. 122–31. In Div 8.6 (SBOp 6/1:115; Luddy 3:432–33), Bernard does associate conversion with entry into a monastery, but the context indicates that he is speaking of conversion of life according to the *Rule.* Yet a recent commentator on twelfth-century education has asserted that the

purpose of Bernard's sermon to the clerics of Paris was to urge them all "to flee the evil city for the safe refuge of the cloister." Stephen C. Ferruolo, *The Origins of the University: The Schools of Paris and Their Critics, 1100–1215* (Stanford, California: Stanford University Press, 1985), p. 47.

52. Ep 94.1; SBOp 7:243–44; James 236–37.

53. *Transitus* is the twelfth-century term. On this, see Douglas Roby, "Philip of Harvengt's Contribution to the Question of Passage from One Religious Order to Another," *Analecta Praemonstratensia* 49 (1973) 69–100. For Bernard, see pp. 74–80. Christopher Holdsworth has suggested that Bernard's view of *transitus* may have changed to a more positive stance in the four years between 1121 and 1125. See his "The Early Writings of Bernard of Clairvaux," *Cîteaux* 45 (1994) 55. This might well be true, but I find Bernard's teaching on the subject to be internally consistent throughout his life, as I trust this section illustrates.

54. The literature on the question is extensive. Useful works include: Jean de la Croix Bouton, "Bernard et l'Ordre de Cluny," in *Bernard de Clairvaux*, pp. 193–217; Adriaan H. Bredero, "Saint Bernard in His Relations with Peter the Venerable," in *Bernardus Magister*, pp. 315–47; F. Cabrol, "Cluny et Cîteaux: Saint Bernard et Pierre le Vénérable," in Association Bourguignonne des Sociétés Savantes (ed.), *Saint Bernard et son temps* (Dijon: au siège de l'Academie, Palais des Etats, 1928–1929), 1:19–28; and M. D. Knowles, *Cistercians & Cluniacs, passim.*

55. Ep 1.11; SBOp 7:9; James 8.

56. Ep 1.9; SBOp 7:8; James 7.

57. Apo 8.16; SBOp 3:95; CF 1:52–53. The contrasting Cistercian life is described in Div 22.5 (SBOp 6/1:173; Luddy 3:545) and Ep 1.4 (SBOp 7:4; James 4).

58. Jean Leclercq, "Introduction" to *The Works of Bernard of Clairvaux*, 1, *Treatises I*, CF 1 (Spencer, Massachusetts: Cistercian Publications, 1970), pp. 21 and 25. See also Leclercq, *Bernard of Clairvaux and the Cistercian Spirit*, p. 14.

59. Leclercq, "Introduction," p. 8, which includes a quotation from Peter's *Letter 161*.

60. Bede K. Lackner, review of Bredero, *Cluny et Cîteaux...*, in *Church History* 73 (1987) 435.

61. Apo 12.30; SBOp 3:107; CF 1:68. The same ambiguity seems to be present in Ep 417; SBOp 8:401–2; James 512–13.

62. Apo 4.7; SBOp 3:87–88; CF 1:42. See Apo 4.8; SBOp 3:88; CF 1:43.

63. Ep 68.3; SBOp 7:167; James 98. See, too, Ep 382.2 (SBOp 8:347–48; James 487–88) and Ep 395.1–2 (SBOp 8:370–71; James 489).

64. Ep 84; SBOp 7:218; James 124. I have followed Leclercq's translation; for this and a penetrating analysis of Bernard's teaching on *transitus,* see *Bernard of Clairvaux and the Cistercian Spirit,* p. 39. Bernard elaborates his thoughts concerning *transitus* in Pre 16.44–46; SBOp 3:283–85; CF 1:138–40.

65. Ep 408; SBOp 8:389; James 507.

66. Ep 442; SBOp 8:420; James 518.

67. See Ep 422; SBOp 8:406; James 515.

68. See Ep 253.3; SBOp 8:151; James 404–5.

69. Ep 83.2; SBOp 7:217–18; James 123–24. See Pre 16.49; SBOp 3:286–87; CF 1:142.

70. Ep 115.1; SBOp 7:294–95; James 179–80.

71. Ep 115.2; SBOp 7:295; James 180.

72. Ep 1.2; SBOp 7:2; James 2.

73. Apo 3.5 and 4.9; SBOp 3:85 and 89; CF 1:39 and 44.

74. Apo 5.10; SBOp 3:90; CF 1:45.

75. Apo 2.4; SBOp 3:83–84; CF 1:37.

76. Apo 2.4; SBOp 3:84; CF 1:37.

77. See Apo 2.4; SBOp 3:84; CF 1:37–38.

78. Apo 6.12; SBOp 3:92; CF 1:48.

79. Apo 1.1; SBOp 3:81; CF 1:34.

80. Apo 1.1; SBOp 3:81–82; CF 1:34–35.

81. Ep 78.3; SBOp 7:203; James 112.

82. Pre 16.47; SBOp 3:285; CF 1:140.

83. Pre 16.47; SBOp 3:285–86; CF 1:140–41.

84. Pre 16.48; SBOp 3:286; CF 1:141.

85. See Jean de la Croix Bouton, "Bernard et les monastères bénédictines non clunisiens," in *Bernard de Clairvaux,* pp. 219–49.

86. See Jean de la Croix Bouton, "Bernard et les Chanoines Réguliers," and "Chanoines et abbayes cisterciennes au temps de saint Bernard," in *Bernard de Clairvaux,* pp. 263–88 and 543–47. See also François Petit, "Bernard et l'Ordre de Prémontré," in *Bernard de Clairvaux,* pp. 289–307; and Henry-Bernard de Warren, "Bernard et l'Ordre de Saint-Victor," in *Bernard de Clairvaux,* pp. 309–26. A more generic treatment may be found in Paschalis Vermeer, "Sint Bernardus en de Orden der reguliere kanunniken van Prémontré, St. Victor en Arrouaise," in *Sint Bernardus van Clairvaux,* pp. 55–64.

87. See Francis Giraudot and Jean de la Croix Bouton, "Bernard et les Gilbertins," in *Bernard de Clairvaux,* pp. 327–38.

88. See Joseph Grillon, "Bernard et les ermites et groupements érémitiques," in *Bernard de Clairvaux,* pp. 251–62.

89. See Ep 11 (SBOp 7:52–60; James 41–48) and Ep 12 (SBOp 7:61–62; James 48–49).

90. SC 9.8; SBOp 1:47; CF 4:59.

91. SC 12.8; SBOp 1:65–66; CF 4:83–84. See also SC 12.10; SBOp 1:66–67; CF 4:85.

92. SC 12.9; SBOp 1:66; CF 4:84.

93. See SC 12.9; SBOp 1:66; CF 4:84–85. See also SC 40.3 (SBOp 2:26; CF 7:201), where a "pure intention and a good conscience will quickly and easily cleanse" Martha from the "dust" gathered in her care for others. Of course, Bernard does recognize that there are bad clerics who "snatch the bride's adornments and use them foully to finance the gratification of their evil desires" (Par 6; SBOp 6/2:295; CF 55:85), but that is another matter altogether.

94. Bernard performs a similar service of instruction for those engaged in active labors who might murmur against contemplatives. See Asspt 3.3; SBOp 5:240; Luddy 3:239–40.

95. Hyperbole is also the basis for Bernard's encouragement of monks in describing their life as a second baptism because of their "perfect renunciation of the world and the singular excellence of their spiritual life." Pre 17.54; SBOp 3:289; CF 1:144. See Feiss, "Theology of Baptism," p. 86.

96. Ep 126.9; SBOp 7:316; James 196.

97. See Div 9.3; SBOp 6/1:120.

98. Ep 238.4; SBOp 8:117; James 278.

99. Fritegotto devotes an entire section (pp. 72–78) of his study of Bernard's ecclesiology to this: "De periculis in vita saeculi." I find this section the least satisfactory part of an otherwise solid work, and this because Fritegotto seems to ignore the interaction between Bernard's rhetoric and his audience.

100. 4 HM 12; SBOp 5:65; Luddy 2:150.

101. Ep 8.1; SBOp 7:47; James 38.

102. Ep 87.3 and 5; SBOp 7:226 and 227; James 131–32. See Ep 319.1–2; SBOp 8:252; James 244.

103. Ep 238.4; SBOp 8:117; James 278. See Ep 142.1; SBOp 7:340; James 219–20.

104. Ep 144.4; SBOp 7:346; James 215.

105. See Ep 237.2–3; SBOp 8:114; James 385–86.

106. See Ep 449; SBOp 8:426; James 285–86.

107. Ep 273.2; SBOp 8:184; James 421.

108. Nat 1.7; SBOp 4:249–50; Luddy 1:388.

109. Bernard uses Paul's distinction between lawful and expedient (1 Cor 6:12) in Hum 10.30; SBOp 3:39; CF 13:59.

110. Tpl 1.2; SBOp 3:215; CF 19:131.

111. Abb 1; SBOp 5:289; Luddy 3:307.

112. See Abb 2; SBOp 5:289–90; Luddy 3:308.

113. See Ep 392; SBOp 8:362; James 495.

114. See Div 40.9; SBOp 6/1:242; Luddy 3:458. See above, p. 7.

115. See Nat 1.7; SBOp 4:249; Luddy 1:388.

116. See Conv 20.36; SBOp 4:113; CF 25:74. For a more complete discussion of the continence demanded of all and the chasity chosen by some—and of the need for both to be expressed in humility—see *Spiritual Teachings,* pp. 161–63.

117. Csi 2.13.22; SBOp 3:429; CF 37:76. One must remember that Bernard is given to hyperbole in correcting the faults of any social group. See above, pp. 94–96 and 98–99.

118. Ep 78.1; SBOp 7:201; James 111.

119. See Ep 6.1; SBOp 7:30; James 25.

120. See Ep 261; SBOp 8:170–71; James 415.

121. Ep 78.11–12; SBOp 7:208–9; James 116–17.

122. Ep 203; SBOp 8:62; James 342.

123. Csi 1.6.7; SBOp 3:402; CF 37:36.

124. Clerics are likewise not to usurp the elaborate dress that is legitimate for laywomen "anxious to please their husbands." See Leclercq, *Women and Saint Bernard of Clairvaux,* p. 16, citing Mor 4; SBOp 7:104.

125. Ep 441; SBOp 8:419; James 517–18.

126. Ep 31; SBOp 7:85–86; James 65.

127. SC 12.3; SBOp 1:61–62; CF 4:79. John's generosity was matched by that of Moses. See SC 12.4; SBOp 1:62–63; CF 4:79–80. Bernard is especially impressed by the gentleness of David. See SC 12.5; SBOp 1:63; CF 4:80–81.

IX. Resolving Some Apparent Inconsistencies

1. An earlier version of some of the material in this section appeared in my "The Chimaera Revisited," *Cîteaux* 38 (1987) 5–13.

2. Robert Fossier, "L'essor économique de Clairvaux," in *Bernard de Clairvaux,* p. 97, n. 12.

3. Leclercq, *Bernard of Clairvaux and the Cistercian Spirit,* p. 37.

4. See, for example, Ep 107.13 (SBOp 7:275–76; James 164) and Conv 21.37 (SBOp 4:113; CF 25:75).

5. See Bernard Jacqueline, "Bernard et le schisme d'Anaclet II," in *Bernard de Clairvaux,* pp. 349–54.

6. See André Seguin, "Bernard et la seconde Croisade," in *Bernard de Clairvaux,* pp. 379–409.

7. See, for example, Ep 243.3–6 (SBOp 8:131–34; James 392–94) and Ep 244 (SBOp 8:134–36; James 394–95).

8. See Ep 35 (SBOp 7:92; James 69) and Ep 97 (SBOp 7:247–48; James 143).

9. Many scholars have seen Bernard primarily in terms of his activity, despite their acknowledgment of the depths of his spiritual teachings. One biographer, Bruno S. James (*Saint Bernard of Clairvaux: An Essay in Biography* [London: Hodder & Stoughton, 1957]), acknowledges that Bernard was a "great mystic," but devotes all but a few pages to his activities outside the cloister. The titles of books and articles, good and bad, learned and popular, bear out this image of Bernard; for example, Paul Mitterre, *Saint Bernard: Um moine arbitre de l'Europe au XIIe siècle* (Genval: Librairie de Lannoy, 1929), or René Dumesnil, *Saint Bernard, homme d'action* (Paris: Desclée, De Brouwer et cie, 1934). There is even a small article entitled "Le dynamisme de saint Bernard" (in *Mélanges saint Bernard: XXIVe Congrès de l'Association Bourguignonne des Sociétés Savants [8e Centenaire de la mort de saint Bernard, Dijon, 1953]* [Dijon: chez M. l'abbé Marilier, n.d.], pp. 219–20) written, appropriately enough, by a French colonel, G. Lélu. The references could be multiplied manyfold. One of the lesser-known Fest-schriften which appeared in 1953 to celebrate the five-hundredth anniversary of Bernard's death was done by the novices of the Cistercian abbey of Achel and bears the title *De monnik van Europas straaten: Sint Bernardus van Clairvaux* ('s-Gravenhage: Pax, 1953). Even those who, like O. Herding, see Bernard as a naive problem solver, still view him as a man in the world; see "Bernard von Clairvaux und die mittelalterlichen Welt," *Geist und Leben* 24 (1951) 106–12. See also M. Louis [Thomas] Merton, "Action and Contemplation in St Bernard," *Coll* 15 (1953) 26–31, 203–16, and 16 (1954) 105–21, reprinted in *Thomas Merton on Saint Bernard,* CS 9 (Kalamazoo, Michigan: Cistercian Publications; London, Oxford: A. R. Mowbray & Co. Ltd., 1980), pp. 21–104.

10. See above, pp. 33–34 and 66–67.

11. Ep 48.1; SBOp 7:137–38; James 79.

12. Ep 48.2; SBOp 7:138; James 80.

13. See above, pp. 70–73.

14. Ep 544; SBOp 8:511–12; James 469.

15. Ep 359; SBOp 8:304–5; James 23–24.

16. See Ep 355; SBOp 8:299; James 348.

17. Ep 256.4; SBOp 8:164–65; James 472.

18. Arnold of Bonneval, *Vita prima* 2.1.3; PL 185:270. I have more or less followed the translation in Ailbe J. Luddy, *Life and Teaching of St. Bernard* (Dublin: M. H. Gill & Son, Ltd., 1950), p. 227.

19. I have expressed my reservations about Arnold's account above, p. 1.

20. Watkin Williams gives a detailed description of the schism and the council, relying always on a multitude of primary sources, in *Saint Bernard of Clairvaux*, pp. 96–158.

21. Ep 124.1–2; SBOp 7:305–6; James 188–89. See also Ep 125 (SBOp 7:307–8; James 189–90) and Ep 126 (SBOp 7:309–19; James 190–99).

22. Ep 280.1; SBOp 8:192; James 425.

23. Ep 365.1; SBOp 8:321; James 465.

24. Ep 144.4; SBOp 7:346; James 215.

25. Par 7; SBOp 6/2:302–3; CF 55:99–100.

26. Ep 166.2; SBOp 7:377–78; James 254.

27. Ep 12; SBOp 7:61–62; James 49. See Ep 145; SBOp 7:347; James 213.

28. Ep 143.1; SBOp 7:342; James 212.

29. Ep 144.1–2; SBOp 7:344–45; James 214.

30. Ep 152; SBOp 7:359; James 228.

31. See Ep 276.3 (SBOp 8:188; James 423–24) and Ep 164.1 (SBOp 7:372–73; James 249–50).

32. Ep 144.4; SBOp 7:346; James 215. See Ep 213; SBOp 8:73; James 354.

33. Ep 52; SBOp 7:144; James 84.

34. Ep 48.3; SBOp 7:139–40; James 81.

35. Ep 46; SBOp 7:135; James 77.

36. Ep 150.3; SBOp 7:355; James 224. See Ep 431; SBOp 8:411–13; James 225–26.

37. Ep 521; SBOp 8:483–84; James 472–73.

38. See Ep 143.2; SBOp 7:342–43; James 212.

39. Ep 143.3; SBOp 7:343; James 213.

40. Ep 13; SBOp 7:62; James 49.

41. Ep 14; SBOp 7:63; James 50. See Ep 20; SBOp 7:70; James 55.

42. See SC 49.6; SBOp 2:76; CF 31:26.

43. Ep 250.4; SBOp 8:147; James 402.

44. Among the abundance of works on Bernard and art, the following are especially useful: Anselme Dimier, "Saint Bernard et l'art," in *Sint Bernardus van Clairvaux*, pp. 295–306; M. Kilian Hufgard, "Saint Bernard of Clairvaux: Friend or Foe of the Arts?" in *Heaven on Earth: Studies in Medieval Cistercian History, IX,* pp. 62–71; Hufgard, *Saint Bernard of Clairvaux: A Theory of Art Formulated from His Writings and Illustrated in Twelfth-Century Works of Art* (Lewiston, New York: The Edwin Mellen Press, 1990); Daniel M. La Corte, "Flawed Portrayals of Bernard of Clairvaux's Attitude Towards Art," *CSQ* 29 (1994) 451–69; La Corte, *Purity of Purpose: The Aesthetics of Bernard of Clairvaux Based on His Monastic Anthropology* (unpublished M. A. thesis, Western Michigan University, 1991); Leclercq, *Bernard of Clairvaux and the Cistercian Spirit,* pp. 18–19; Elizabeth Melczer and Eileen Soldwedel, "Monastic Goals in the Aesthetics of Saint Bernard," in Meredith P. Lillich (ed.), *Studies in Cistercian Art and Architecture, I,* CS 66 (Kalamazoo, Michigan: Cistercian Publications, 1982), pp. 31–44; Conrad Rudolph, "The 'Principal Founders' and the Early Artistic Legislation of Cîteaux," in Meredith Parsons Lillich (ed.), *Studies in Cistercian Art and Architecture, III,* CS 89 (Kalamazoo, Michigan: Cistercian Publications, 1987), pp. 1–45; Rudolph, "The Scholarship on Bernard of Clairvaux's Apologia," *Cîteaux* 40 (1989) 69–111; Rudolf, *The "Things of Greater Importance": Bernard of Clairvaux's Apologia and the Medieval Attitude Toward Art* (Philadelphia: University of Pennsylvania Press, 1990) (see my review in *Church History* 62 [1993] 549–50); Emero Stiegman, "Saint Bernard: The Aesthetics of Authenticity," in Meredith Parsons Lillich (ed.), *Studies in Cistercian Art and Architecture, II,* CS 69 (Kalamazoo, Michigan: Cistercian Publications Inc., 1984), pp. 1–13; and Henry-Bernard de Warren, "Bernard et les premiers Cisterciens face au problème de l'art," in *Bernard de Clairvaux,* pp. 487–534. Some material in this section is contained in my "The Social Theory of Bernard of Clairvaux," pp. 46–47.

45. Apo 12.28; SBOp 3:104; CF 1:63.

46. Apo 12.28; SBOp 3:104; CF 1:64.

47. Apo 12.28; SBOp 3:105; CF 1:65.

48. Apo 12.28; SBOp 3:105; CF 1:65.

49. Apo 12.28; SBOp 3:105–6; CF 1:65–66.

50. Ep 243.4; SBOp 8:132; James 392–93.

51. Apo 12.28; SBOp 3:104–5; CF 1:64.
52. Apo 12.29; SBOp 3:106; CF 1:66.
53. V Mal 28.63; SBOp 3:368; CF 10:80.
54. SC 46.1 and 4; SBOp 2:56 and 57–58; CF 7:241 and 243.
55. See above, p. 3.
56. See above, pp. 5–6.

Bibliography

I. Primary Sources

A. The Works of Bernard of Clairvaux

1. Critical Edition

Jean Leclercq et al. (eds.). *Sancti Bernardi opera*. Roma: Editiones Cistercienses, 8 vols. in 9, 1957–1977.

2. Individual Works and Translations

Apologia ad Guillelmum abbatum. Opera 3:81–108.
> Trans.: *An Apology to Abbot William*. Trans. Michael Casey; intro. Jean Leclercq. The Works of Bernard of Clairvaux 1; Treatises I. Cistercian Fathers 1. Spencer, Massachusetts: Cistercian Publications, 1970, pp. 33–69.

De consideratione ad Eugenium papam. Opera 3:393–493.
> Trans.: *Five Books on Consideration: Advice to a Pope*. Trans. John D. Anderson and Elizabeth T. Kennan. The Works of Bernard of Clairvaux 13. Cistercian Fathers 37. Kalamazoo, Michigan: Cistercian Publications, 1976.

Epistolae. Opera 7 and 8.
> Trans.: *The Letters of St. Bernard of Clairvaux*. Trans. Bruno Scott James. London: Burns Oates, 1953; reprint Kalamazoo, Michigan: Cistercian Publications, 1998.

> *Letter to Abbot Guy and the Monks of Montiéramey*. Trans. Martinus Cawley. The Works of Bernard of Clairvaux 1; Treatises I. Cistercian Fathers 1. Spencer, Massachusetts: Cistercian Publications, 1970, pp. 180–82.

Liber ad milites Templi de laude novae militiae. Opera 3:213–39.
> Trans.: *In Praise of the New Knighthood*. Trans. M. Conrad
> Greenia; intro. R. J. Zwi Werblowsky. The Works of Bernard of
> Clairvaux 7; Treatises III. Cistercian Fathers 19. Kalamazoo,
> Michigan: Cistercian Publications Inc., 1977, pp. 127–67.

Liber de diligendo Deo. Opera 3:119–54.
> Trans.: *On Loving God*. Trans. and intro. Robert Walton. The
> Works of Bernard of Clairvaux 5; Treatises II. Cistercian Fathers
> 13. Washington, D.C.: Cistercian Publications, 1974, pp. 91–132.
> Reprinted, with *An Analytical Commentary* by Emero Stiegman,
> as Cistercian Fathers 13 B. Kalamazoo, Michigan: Cistercian Pub-
> lications Inc., 1995.

Liber de gradibus humilitatis et superbiae. Opera 3:13–59.
> Trans.: *The Steps of Humility and Pride*. Trans. M. Ambrose Con-
> way; intro. M. Basil Pennington. The Works of Bernard of Clair-
> vaux 5; Treatises II. Cistercian Fathers 13. Washington, D.C.:
> Cistercian Publications, 1974, pp. 25–82.

Liber de gratia et libero arbitrio. Opera 3:165–203.
> Trans.: *On Grace and Free Choice*. Trans. Daniel O'Donovan;
> intro. Bernard McGinn. The Works of Bernard of Clairvaux 7;
> Treatises III. Cistercian Fathers 19. Kalamazoo, Michigan: Cis-
> tercian Publications Inc., 1977, pp. 51–111.

Liber de praecepto et dispensatione. Opera 3:254–94.
> Trans.: *Monastic Obligations and Abbatial Authority: Saint
> Bernard's Book on Precept and Dispensation*. Trans. Conrad
> Greenia; intro. Jean Leclercq. The Works of Bernard of Clair-
> vaux 1; Treatises I. Cistercian Fathers 1. Spencer, Massachusetts:
> Cistercian Publications, 1970, pp. 103–50.

Parabolae. Opera 6/2:261–303.
> Trans.: *The Parables*. Trans. and intro. Michael Casey. Cistercian
> Fathers 55. Kalamazoo, Michigan: Cistercian Publications, 2000,
> pp. 9–102.

Sententiae. Opera 6/2:7–255.
> Trans.: *The Sentences*. Trans. Francis R. Swietek; intro. John R.
> Sommerfeldt. Cistercian Fathers 55. Kalamazoo, Michigan: Cis-
> tercian Publications, 2000, pp. 103–458.

Sermo ad clericos de conversione. Opera 4:69–116.
> Trans.: *On Conversion, A Sermon to Clerics.* Trans. and intro. Marie-Bernard Saïd. In *Sermons on Conversion.* Cistercian Fathers 25. Kalamazoo, Michigan: Cistercian Publications, 1981, pp. 31– 79.

Sermones de diversis. Opera 6/1:73–406.
> Note: a few of these sermons, titled *Miscellaneous Sermons,* are translated in *St. Bernard's Sermons for the Seasons & Principal Festivals of the Year.* Trans. A Priest of Mount Melleray [Ailbe J. Luddy]. Reprint, Westminster, Maryland: The Carroll Press, 3 vols., 1950, 3:397–552.

Sermones per annum. Opera 4:161–492; 5; and 6/1:9–55.
> Trans.: *St. Bernard's Sermons for the Seasons & Principal Festivals of the Year.* Trans. A Priest of Mount Melleray [Ailbe J. Luddy]. Reprint, Westminster, Maryland: The Carroll Press, 3 vols., 1950.

> Note: a translation of some of these sermons, *Sermones in Quadragesima de psalmo "Qui habitat"* (*Opera* 4:383–492), appears as *Lenten Sermons on the Psalm "He Who Dwells"* in *Sermons on Conversion.* Trans. Marie-Bernard Saïd. Cistercian Fathers 25. Kalamazoo, Michigan: Cistercian Publications, 1981, pp. 111–261. The *Sermon on the Passing of Saint Malachy the Bishop* (*In transitu sancti Malachiae episcopi; Opera* 5:417–23) and the *Homily on the Anniversary of the Death of Saint Malachy* (*De sancto Malachia; Opera* 6/1:50–55) are translated in *The Life and Death of Saint Malachy the Irishman.* Trans. Robert T. Meyer. Cistercian Fathers 10. Kalamazoo, Michigan: Cistercian Publications, 1978, pp. 95–112. Nineteen of the liturgical sermons are translated in *Sermons for the Summer Season: Liturgical Sermons from Rogationtide and Pentecost.* Trans. Beverly Mayne Kienzle and James Jarzembowski. Cistercian Fathers 53. Kalamazoo, Michigan: Cistercian Publications, 1991.

Sermones super Cantica canticorum. Opera 1 and 2.
> Trans.: Sermons 1–20: *On the Song of Songs I.* Trans. Kilian Walsh; intro. M. Corneille Halflants. The Works of Bernard of Clairvaux 2. Cistercian Fathers 4. Kalamazoo, Michigan: Cistercian Publications Inc., 1981 (first printing 1971).

Sermons 21–46: *On the Song of Songs II.* Trans. Kilian Walsh; intro. Jean Leclercq. The Works of Bernard of Clairvaux 3. Cistercian Fathers 7. Kalamazoo, Michigan: Cistercian Publications, 1976.

Sermons 47–66: *On the Song of Songs III.* Trans. Kilian Walsh and Irene M. Edmonds; intro. Emero Stiegman. Cistercian Fathers 31. Kalamazoo, Michigan: Cistercian Publications, 1979.

Sermons 67–86: *On the Song of Songs IV.* Trans. Irene Edmonds; intro. Jean Leclercq. Cistercian Fathers 40. Kalamazoo, Michigan: Cistercian Publications, 1980.

Sermones in laudibus Virginis Matris [Homiliae super "Missus est" in laudibus Virginis Matris]. Opera 4:13–58.
> Trans.: *Four Homilies in Praise of the Virgin Mother.* Trans. Marie-Bernard Saïd and Grace Perigo; intro. Chrysogonus Waddell. In *Magnificat: Homilies in Praise of the Blessed Virgin Mary.* Cistercian Fathers 18. Kalamazoo, Michigan: Cistercian Publications Inc., 1979, pp. 1–58.

Vita sancti Malachiae episcopi. Opera 3:307–78.
> Trans.: *The Life of Saint Malachy.* Trans. Robert T. Meyer. In *The Life and Death of Saint Malachy the Irishman.* Cistercian Fathers 10. Kalamazoo, Michigan: Cistercian Publications, 1978, pp. 9–93.

B. Works by Other Authors

Arnold of Bonneval. *Sancti Bernardi abbatis Clarae-Vallensis vita et res gestae [Vita prima], Liber secundus.* In J.-P. Migne (ed.), *Patrologia latina.* Paris: apud J.-P. Migne editorem, 1841. Vol. 185, cols. 267–302.

Benedict of Nursia. *Regula monachorum.* Ed. Cuthbertus Butler. 3rd ed., St. Louis: B. Herder Book Co., 1935.
> Trans.: *Households of God: The Rule of St Benedict with Explanations for Monks and Lay-people Today.* Trans. David Parry. Cistercian Studies 39. Kalamazoo, Michigan: Cistercian Publications, 1980.

Geoffrey of Auxerre. *Fragmenta de vita et miraculis s. Bernardi.* Ed. Robert Lechat. In *Analecta Bollandiana* 50 (1932) 83–122.

Trans. (in part): *Bernard of Clairvaux: Early Biographies*, 2, *By Geoffrey and Others*. Trans. Martinus Cawley. Lafayette, Oregon: Guadalupe Translations, 1990.

Odo of Deuil. *De profectione Ludovici VII in orientem*. Ed. and trans. Virginia Gingerick Berry. New York: W. W. Norton & Company Inc., 1948.

Otto of Freising. *Gesta Friderici I. imperatoris*. In G. Waitz and B. de Simpson (eds.), *Monumenta Germaniae historica, Scriptores rerum Germanicarum in usum scholarum...*, 46. 3rd ed., Hannover, Leipzig: Impensis Bibliopolii Hahniani, 1912, reprint 1978, pp. 9–161.

> Trans.: *The Deeds of Frederick Barbarossa*. Trans. Charles Christopher Mierow. New York: W. W. Norton & Company, Inc., 1953.

Sancti Bernardi abbatis Clarae-Vallensis vita et res gestae, Liber sextus seu miracula a sancto Bernardo per Germaniam, Belgium Galliamque patrata, anno 1146, pars secunda. In J.-P. Migne (ed.), *Patrologia latina*. Paris: apud J.-P. Migne editorem, 1841. Vol. 185, cols. 383–416.

II. SECONDARY SOURCES

Auberger, Jean-Baptiste. *L'unanimité cistercienne primitive: Mythe ou realité?* Achel: Administration de Cîteaux: Commentarii Cistercienses; Editions Sine Parvulos VBVB, 1986.

Bamberger, John Eudes. "The Influence of St Bernard." *Cistercian Studies* 25 (1990) 104–14.

Berry, Virginia G. "The Second Crusade." In *A History of the Crusades* (ed. Kenneth M. Setton), I, *The First Hundred Years* (ed. Marshall W. Baldwin). Madison, Milwaukee, and London: The University of Wisconsin Press, 1969, pp. 463–512.

Bhaldraith, Eoin de. "Jean Leclercq's Attitude Toward War." In E. Rozanne Elder (ed.), *The Joy of Learning and the Love of God: Studies in Honor of Jean Leclercq*. Cistercian Studies 160. Kalamazoo, Michigan; Spencer, Massachusetts: Cistercian Publications, 1995, pp. 217–37.

Bouton, Jean de la Croix. "Bernard et les Chanoines Réguliers." In *Bernard de Clairvaux*. Commission d'histoire de l'Ordre de Cîteaux, 3. Paris: Editions Alsatia, 1953, pp. 263–88.

———. "Bernard et les monastères bénédictines non clunisiens." In *Bernard de Clairvaux*. Commission d'histoire de l'Ordre de Cîteaux, 3. Paris: Editions Alsatia, 1953, pp. 219–49.

————. "Bernard et l'Ordre de Cluny." In *Bernard de Clairvaux*. Commission d'histoire de l'Ordre de Cîteaux, 3. Paris: Editions Alsatia, 1953, pp. 193–217.

————. "Chanoines et abbayes cisterciennes au temps de saint Bernard." In *Bernard de Clairvaux*. Commission d'histoire de l'Ordre de Cîteaux, 3. Paris: Editions Alsatia, 1953, pp. 543–47.

Bredero, Adriaan H. "Saint Bernard in His Relations with Peter the Venerable." In John R. Sommerfeldt (ed.), *Bernardus Magister: Papers Presented at the Nonacentenary Celebration of the Birth of Saint Bernard of Clairvaux, Sponsored by the Institute of Cistercian Studies, Western Michigan University, 10–13 May 1990*. Cistercian Studies 135. Kalamazoo, Michigan: Cistercian Publications; Saint-Nicolas-lès-Cîteaux: Cîteaux: Commentarii Cistercienses, 1992, pp. 315–47.

Bynum, Caroline Walker. *Jesus as Mother: Studies in the Spirituality of the High Middle Ages*. Berkeley, Los Angeles, London: University of California Press, 1984.

Cabrol, F. "Cluny et Cîteaux: Saint Bernard et Pierre le Vénérable." In Association Bourguignonne des Sociétés Savantes (ed.), *Saint Bernard et son temps*. Dijon: au siège de l'Academie, Palais des États, 1928–1929, 1:19–28.

Casey, Michael. "The Meaning of Poverty for Bernard of Clairvaux." *Cistercian Studies Quarterly* 33 (1998) 427–38.

Congar, Yves. "Die Ekklesiologie des hl. Bernhard." In Joseph Lortz (ed.), *Bernard von Clairvaux, Mönch und Mystiker: Internationaler Bernhardkongress, Mainz 1953*. Veröffentlichungen des Instituts für europäische Geschichte Mainz, 6. Wiesbaden: Franz Steiner GmbH, 1955, pp. 76–119.

Constable, Giles. *The Reformation of the Twelfth Century*. Cambridge: Cambridge University Press, 1996.

Dimier, Anselme. "Saint Bernard et l'art." In *Sint Bernardus van Clairvaux: Gedenkboek door monniken van de noord- en zuidnederlandse cisterciënser abdijen samengesteld bij het achtste eeuwfeest van Sint Bernardus' dood, 20 Augustus 1153–1953*. Rotterdam: N.V. Uitgeverij De Forel, 1953, pp. 295–306.

Dumesnil, René. *Saint Bernard, homme d'action*. Paris: Desclée, De Brouwer et cie, 1934.

Feiss, Hugh. "St Bernard's Theology of Baptism and the Monastic Life." *Cistercian Studies* 25 (1990) 79–91.

Ferruolo, Stephen C. *The Origins of the University: The Schools of Paris and Their Critics, 1100–1215*. Stanford, California: Stanford University Press, 1985.

Fossier, Robert. "L'essor économique de Clairvaux." In *Bernard de Clairvaux*. Commission d'histoire de l'Ordre de Cîteaux, 3. Paris: Editions Alsatia, 1953, pp. 95–114.

Fritegotto, Raphael. *De vocatione christiana s. Bernardi doctrina*. Studia Antoniana, 15. Roma: Pontificum Athenaeum Antonianum, 1961.

Giraudot, Francis, and Jean de la Croix Bouton. "Bernard et les Gilbertines." In *Bernard de Clairvaux*. Commission d'histoire de l'Ordre de Cîteaux, 3. Paris: Editions Alsatia, 1953, pp. 327–38.

Grillon, Joseph. "Bernard et les ermites et groupements érémitiques." In *Bernard de Clairvaux*. Commission d'histoire de l'Ordre de Cîteaux, 3. Paris: Editions Alsatia, 1953, pp. 251–62.

Herding, O. "Bernhard von Clairvaux und die mittelalterlichen Welt." *Geist und Leben* 24 (1951) 106–12.

Hermans, Vincentius. "De h. Bernardus en de stichters van Cîteaux." In *Sint Bernardus van Clairvaux: Gedenkboek door monniken van de noord- en zuidnederlandse cisterciënser abdijen samengesteld bij het achtste eeuwfeest van Sint Bernardus' dood, 20 Augustus 1153–1953*. Rotterdam: N.V. Uitgeverij De Forel, 1953, pp. 39–54.

Holdsworth, Christopher. "The Early Writings of Bernard of Clairvaux." *Cîteaux: Commentarii cistercienses* 45 (1994) 21–61.

Hufgard, M. Kilian. "Saint Bernard of Clairvaux: Friend or Foe of the Arts?" In E. Rozanne Elder (ed.), *Heaven on Earth: Studies in Medieval Cistercian History, IX*. Cistercian Studies 68. Kalamazoo, Michigan: Cistercian Pubications, 1983, pp. 62–71.

———. *Saint Bernard of Clairvaux: A Theory of Art Formulated from His Writings and Illustrated in Twelfth-Century Works of Art*. Lewiston, New York: The Edwin Mellen Press, 1990.

Jacqueline, Bernard. "Bernard et le schisme d'Anaclet II." In *Bernard de Clairvaux*. Commission d'histoire de l'Ordre de Cîteaux, 3. Paris: Editions Alsatia, 1953, pp. 349–54.

———. "Épiscopat et papauté chez Saint Bernard de Clairvaux." *Collectanea Cisterciensia* 34 (1972) 218–29.

———. "Saint Grégoire le Grand et l'eccésiologie de saint Bernard." *Collectanea Cisterciensia* 36 (1974) 69–73.

James, Bruno S. *Saint Bernard of Clairvaux: An Essay in Biography*. London: Hodder & Stoughton, 1957.

Kahl, Hans-Dietrich. "Crusade Eschatology as Seen by St. Bernard in the Years 1146 to 1148." In Michael Gervers (ed.), *The Second Crusade and the Cistercians*. New York: St. Martin's Press, 1992, pp. 35–47.

————. "Die Kreuzzugseschatologie Bernhards von Clairvaux und ihre mis-
siongeschichtliche Auswirkung." In Dieter R. Bauer and Gottard Fuchs
(eds.), *Bernhard von Clairvaux und der Beginn der Moderne*. Innsbruck, Wien: Tyrolia-Verlag, 1996, pp. 262–315.

Kennan, Elizabeth T. "Antithesis and Argument in the *De consideratione*."
In M. Basil Pennington (ed.), *Bernard of Clairvaux: Studies Presented to
Dom Jean Leclercq*. Cistercian Studies 23. Washington, D.C.: Cistercian
Publications, 1973, pp. 91–109.

————. "The 'De consideratione' of St. Bernard of Clairvaux and the Papacy
in the Mid-Twelfth Century: A Review of Scholarship." *Traditio* 23
(1967) 73–115.

Knowles, M. D. *Cistercians & Cluniacs: The Controversy Between St. Ber-
nard and Peter the Venerable*. Friends of Dr. William's Library, Ninth
Lecture, 1955. London, New York, Toronto: Geoffry Cumberlege;
Oxford University Press, 1955.

Lackner, Bede K. "The Monastic Life According to Saint Bernard." In John
R. Sommerfeldt (ed.), *Studies in Medieval Cistercian History, II*. Cistercian Studies 24. Kalamazoo, Michigan: Cistercian Publications, 1976,
pp. 49–62.

————. "The Priestly Ideal of Saint Bernard." *The American Ecclesiastical
Review* 140 (1959) 237–44.

————. Review of Adriaan H. Bredero, *Cluny et Cîteaux au douzième siècle:
L'histoire d'une controverse monastique* (Maarsen: Academic Publishers
Associated; Amsterdam: Holland University Press, 1985). In *The Amer-
ican Catholic Historical Review* 73 (1987) 435–36.

————. "Saint Bernard: On Bishops and Rome." *The American Benedictine
Review* 40 (1989) 380–82.

La Corte, Daniel M. "Flawed Portrayals of Bernard of Clairvaux's Attitude
Towards Art." *Cistercian Studies Quarterly* 29 (1994) 451–69.

————. *Purity of Purpose: The Aesthetics of Bernard of Clairvaux Based on
His Monastic Anthropology*. Unpublished M.A. thesis, Western Michigan
University, 1991.

Leclercq, Jean. *Bernard of Clairvaux and the Cistercian Spirit*. Trans. Claire
Lavoie. Cistercian Studies 16. Kalamazoo, Michigan: Cistercian Publications, 1976.

————. "Does St Bernard Have a Specific Message for Nuns?" In John A.
Nichols and Lillian Thomas Shank (eds.), *Medieval Religious Women, I,
Distant Echoes*. Cistercian Studies 71. Kalamazoo, Michigan: Cistercian
Publications Inc., 1984, pp. 269–78.

———. "L'hérésie d'après les écrits de s. Bernard de Clairvaux." In W. Lourdaux and D. Verhelst (eds.), *The Concept of Heresy in the Middle Ages (11th–13th C.): Proceedings of the International Conference, Louvain, May 13–16, 1973.* Mediaevalia Lovaniensia, Series 1, Studies 4. Louvain: University Press; The Hague: Martinus Nijhoff, 1976, pp. 12–26.

———. "Introducton" to *Cistercians and Cluniacs: St Bernard's Apologia to Abbot William.* In *The Works of Bernard of Clairvaux* 1; *Treatises I.* Cistercian Fathers 1. Spencer, Massachusetts: Cistercian Publications, 1970, pp. 3–30.

———. *Monks and Love in Twelfth-Century France: Psycho-Historical Essays.* Oxford: at the Clarendon Press, 1979.

———. *Monks on Marriage: A Twelfth-Century View.* New York: The Seabury Press, 1982.

———. "Saint Bernard on the Church." *Downside Review* 85 (1967) 274–94.

———. "St Bernard on Confession." *Cistercian Studies* 4 (1969) 199–212.

———. "Saint Bernard's Attitude Toward War." In John R. Sommerfeldt (ed.), *Studies in Medieval Cistercian History, II.* Cistercian Studies 24. Kalamazoo, Michigan: Cistercian Publications, 1976, pp. 1–39.

———. *Women and Saint Bernard of Clairvaux.* Trans. Marie-Bernard Saïd. Cistercian Studies 104. Kalamazoo, Michigan: Cistercian Publications, 1989.

Lélu, G. "Le dynamisme de saint Bernard." In *Mélanges saint Bernard: XXIVe Congrès de l'Association Bourguignonne de Sociétés Savantes (8e Centenaire de la morte de saint Bernard, Dijon, 1953).* Dijon: chez M. l'abbé Marilier, n.d., pp. 219–20.

Luddy, Ailbe J. *Life and Teachings of St. Bernard.* Dublin: M. H. Gill & Son, Ltd., 1950.

Maddux, J. S. "St. Bernard as Hagiographer." *Cîteaux: Commentarii cistercienses* 27 (1976) 85–108.

McCaffery, Hugh. "The Basics of Monastic Living in St Bernard." *Cistercian Studies* 25 (1990) 157–62.

McGinn, Bernard. "Saint Bernard and Eschatology." In M. Basil Pennington (ed.), *Bernard of Clairvaux: Studies Presented to Dom Jean Leclercq.* Cistercian Studies 23. Washington, D.C.: Cistercian Publications, 1973, pp. 161–85.

Melczer, Elizabeth, and Eileen Soldwedel. "Monastic Goals in the Aesthetics of Saint Bernard." In Meredith P. Lillich (ed.), *Studies in Cistercian Art and Architecture, I.* Cistercian Studies 66. Kalamazoo, Michigan: Cistercian Publications, 1982, pp. 31–44.

Merton, M. Louis [Thomas]. "Action and Contemplation in St Bernard." *Collectanea Cisterciensia* 15 (1953) 26–31, 203–16, and 16 (1954) 105–21. Reprinted in *Thomas Merton on Saint Bernard.* Cistercian Studies 9. Kalamazoo, Michigan: Cistercian Publications; London, Oxford: A. R. Mowbray & Co. Ltd., 1980, pp. 21–104.

———. "St. Bernard, Monk and Apostle." *Cross and Crown* 5 (1953) 251–63.

Miterre, Paul. *Saint Bernard: Un moine arbitre de l'Europe au XIIe siècle.* Genval: Libraire de Lannoy, 1929.

Newman, Martha G. *The Boundaries of Charity: Cistercian Culture and Ecclesiastical Reform.* Figurae: Reading Medieval Culture. Stanford, California: Stanford University Press, 1996.

Noviciaat van de Achelse Kluis (ed.). *De monnik van Europa's straaten, Sint Bernardus van Clairvaux.* s'Gravenhage: Pax, 1953.

Paulsell, William O. "Saint Bernard on the Duties of the Christian Prince." In John R. Sommerfeldt (ed.), *Studies in Medieval Cistercian History, II.* Cistercian Studies 24. Kalamazoo, Michigan: Cistercian Publications, 1976, pp. 63–74.

Petit, François. "Bernard et l'Ordre de Prémontré." In *Bernard de Clairvaux.* Commission d'histoire de l'Ordre de Cîteaux, 3. Paris: Editions Alsatia, 1953, pp. 289–307.

Phillips, Paschal. "The Presence—and Absence—of Bernard of Clairvaux in the Twelfth-Century Chronicles." In John R. Sommerfeldt (ed.), *Bernardus Magister: Papers Presented at the Nonacentenary Celebration of the Birth of Saint Bernard of Clairvaux, Sponsored by the Institute of Cistercian Studies, Western Michigan University, 10–13 May 1990.* Kalamazoo, Michigan: Cistercian Publications; Saint-Nicolas-lès-Cîteaux: Cîteaux: Commentarii Cistercienses, 1992, pp. 35–53.

Principe, Walter H. "Monastic, Episcopal, and Apologetic Theology of the Papacy, 1150–1250." In Christopher Ryan (ed.), *The Religious Roles of the Papacy: Ideals and Realities, 1150–1300.* Papers in Mediaeval Studies 8. Toronto: Pontifical Institute of Mediaeval Studies, 1989, pp. 117–70.

Renna, Thomas. "The City in Early Cistercian Thought." *Cîteaux: Commentarii cistercienses* 34 (1983) 5–19.

———. "Early Cistercian Attitudes Toward War in Historical Perspective." *Cîteaux: Commentarii cistercienses* 31 (1980) 119–29.

————. "St Bernard's View of the Episcopacy in Historical Perspective, 400–1150." *Cistercian Studies* 15 (1980) 39–49.

————. "The Wilderness and the Cistercians." *Cistercian Studies Quarterly* 30 (1995) 179–89.

Richard, Jean. "Le milieu familial." In *Bernard de Clairvaux*. Commission d'histoire de l'Ordre de Cîteaux, 3. Paris: Editions Alsatia, 1953, pp. 3–15.

Rissetto, Marion. "Fish for the Pond: The Recruitment Dynamic of Bernard of Clairvaux." *Word and Spirit: A Monastic Review* 12 (1990) 148–61.

Roby, Douglas. "Philip of Harvengt's Contribution to the Question of Passage from One Religious Order to Another." *Analecta Praemonstratensia* 49 (1973) 69–100.

Rudolph, Conrad. "The 'Principal Founders' and the Early Artistic Legislation of Cîteaux." In Meredith Parsons Lillich (ed.), *Studies in Cistercian Art and Architecture III*. Cistercian Studies 89. Kalamazoo, Michigan: Cistercian Publications, 1987, pp. 1–45.

————. "The Scholarship on Bernard of Clairvaux's *Apologia*." *Cîteaux: Commentarii cistercienses* 40 (1989) 69–111.

————. *The "Things of Greater Importance": Bernard of Clairvaux's* Apologia *and the Medieval Attitude Toward Art*. Philadelphia: University of Pennsylvania Press, 1990.

Russel, Edith. "Bernard et les dames de son temps." In *Bernard de Clairvaux*. Commission d'histoire de l'Ordre de Cîteaux, 3. Paris: Editions Alsatia, 1953, pp. 411–25.

Saint Bernard théologien: Acts du Congrès de Dijon, 15–19 Septembre 1953 (= *Analecta Sacri Ordinis Cisterciensis* 9 [1953] fasc. 3–4). 2nd ed., Roma: Editiones Cisterciensis, 1954.

Seguin, André. "Bernard et la seconde Croisade." In *Bernard de Clairvaux*. Commission d'histoire de l'Ordre de Cîteaux, 3. Paris: Editions Alsatia, 1953, pp. 379–409.

Sommerfeldt, John R. "Bernard of Clairvaux's Abbot: Both Daniel and Noah." In Francis R. Swietek and John R. Sommerfeldt (eds.), *Studiosorum speculum: Studies in Honor of Louis J. Lekai, O.Cist.* Cistercian Studies 141. Kalamazoo, Michigan: Cistercian Publications, 1993, pp. 355–62.

————. "Bernard of Clairvaux on Love and Marriage." *Cistercian Studies Quarterly* 30 (1995) 141–46.

————. "Bernard of Clairvaux as Sermon Writer and Sentence Speaker." The introduction to Bernard of Clairvaux, *The Sentences*. Trans. Francis R.

Swietek. Cistercian Fathers 55. Kalamazoo, Michigan: Cistercian Publications, 2000, pp. 105–14.

——. "The Bernardine Reform and the Crusading Spirit." *The Catholic Historical Review* 86 (2000) 567–78.

——. "Charismatic and Gregorian Leadership in the Thought of Bernard of Clairvaux." In M. Basil Pennington (ed.), *Bernard of Clairvaux: Studies Presented to Dom Jean Leclercq.* Cistercian Studies 23. Washington, D.C.: Cistercian Publications, 1973, pp. 73–90.

——. "The Chimaera Revisited." *Cîteaux: Commentarii cistercienses* 38 (1987) 5–13.

——. "Epistemological and Social Hierarchies: A Potential Reconciliation of Some Inconsistencies in Bernard's Thought." *Cîteaux: Commentarii cistercienses* 31 (1980) 83–92. Reprinted in Marion Leathers Kuntz and Paul Grimley Kuntz (eds.), *Jacob's Ladder and the Tree of Life: Concepts of Hierarchy and the Great Chain of Being.* American University Studies, Series 5, Philosophy 14. New York, Bern, Frankfurt am Main, Paris: Peter Lang, 1987, pp. 141–51.

——. "The Intellectual Life According to Saint Bernard." *Cîteaux: Commentarii cistercienses* 25 (1974) 249–56.

——. "The Monk and Monastic Life in the Thought of Bernard of Clairvaux." *Word and Spirit: A Monastic Review* 12 (1990) 43–53.

——. Review of Baldwin of Ford, *Spiritual Tractates,* trans. David N. Bell, Cistercian Fathers 38 and 41 (Kalamazoo, Michigan: Cistercian Publications Inc., 2 vols., 1986). In *Speculum* 64 (1989) 384–85.

——. Review of Conrad Rudolph, *The "Things of Greater Importance": Bernard of Clairvaux's Apologia and the Medieval Attitude Toward Art* (Philadelphia: University of Pennsylvania Press, 1990). In *Church History* 62 (1993) 549–50.

——. "The Social Theory of Bernard of Clairvaux." In Joseph F. O'Callaghan (ed.), *Studies in Medieval Cistercian History Presented to Jeremiah F. O'Sullivan.* Cistercian Studies 13. Spencer, Massachusetts: Cistercian Publications, 1971, pp. 35–48.

——. *The Spiritual Teachings of Bernard of Clairvaux.* An Intellectual History of the Early Cistercian Order, [1]. Cistercian Studies 125. Kalamazoo, Michigan: Cistercian Publications, 1991.

——. "Vassals of the Lord and Ministers of God: The Role of the Governing Class in the Ecclesiology of Bernard of Clairvaux." *Cistercian Studies Quarterly* 29 (1994) 55–60.

Stiegman, Emero. "Saint Bernard: The Aesthetics of Authenticity." In Meredith Parsons Lillich (ed.), *Studies in Cistercian Art and Architecture, II.*

Cistercian Studies 69. Kalamazoo, Michigan: Cistercian Publications Inc., 1984, pp. 1–13.

Ver Bust, Richard. "Papal Ministry: A Source of Theology, Bernard of Clairvaux's Letters." In E. Rozanne Elder (ed.), *Heaven on Earth: Studies in Medieval Cistercian History, IX.* Cistercian Studies 68. Kalamazoo, Michigan: Cistercian Publications, 1983, pp. 55–61.

Vermeer, Paschalis. "Sint Bernardus en de Orden der reguliere kanunniken van Prémontré, St. Victor en Arrouaise." In *Sint Bernardus van Clairvaux: Gedenkboek door monniken van de noord- en zuidnederlandse cistercënser abdijen samengesteld bij het achtste eeuwfeest van Sint Bernardus' dood, 20 Augustus 1153–1953.* Rotterdam: N.V. Uitgeverij De Forel, 1953, pp. 55–64.

Warren, Henry-Bernard de. "Bernard et l'épiscopat." In *Bernard de Clairvaux.* Commission d'histoire de l'Ordre de Cîteaux, 3. Paris: Editions Alsatia, 1953, pp. 627–47.

———. "Bernard et l'Ordre de Saint-Victor." In *Bernard de Clairvaux.* Commission d'histoire de l'Ordre de Cîteaux, 3. Paris: Editions Alsatia, 1953, pp. 309–26.

———. "Bernard et les premiers Cisterciens face au problème de l'art." In *Bernard de Clairvaux.* Commission d'histoire de l'Ordre de Cîteaux, 3. Paris: Editions Alsatia, 1953, pp. 487–534.

———. "Bernard, les princes et la société féodal." In *Bernard de Clairvaux.* Commission d'histoire de l'Ordre de Cîteaux, 3. Paris: Editions Alsatia, 1953, pp. 649–57.

White, Hayden V. "The Gregorian Ideal and Saint Bernard of Clairvaux." *Journal of the History of Ideas* 21 (1960) 321–48.

Wieruszowski, Helene. "Roger II of Sicily, *Rex-Tyrannus,* in Twelfth-Century Political Thought." *Speculum* 38 (1963) 46–78.

Williams, Watkin. *Saint Bernard of Clairvaux.* Manchester: Manchester University Press, 1935, reprint 1953.

Wolter, Hans. "Bernhard von Clairvaux und die Laien: Aussagen der monastischen Theologie über Ort und Berufung des Laien in der erlösten Welt." *Scholastik* 34 (1959) 161–89.

Index

Other books in The Newman Press series:

ANCIENT CHRISTIAN WRITERS
(59-volume series)

FROM APOSTLES TO BISHOPS
by Francis A. Sullivan

THE DIDACHE
by Aaron Milavec

THE RULE OF SAINT BENEDICT
by Mayeul de Dreuille, O.S.B.

BERNARD OF CLAIRVAUX ON THE LIFE OF THE MIND
by John R. Sommerfeldt